My Bestie

I cannot tell you how much I love you!

## THERE IS ONLY PLAN A

You are the ultimate support, cherished friend and beauty! Allow Plan A to be your guide to all things miraculous!

Love,
Kay

# THERE IS ONLY PLAN A

*A Journey Toward Self-Discovery and Renewed Purpose*

KLAY S. WILLIAMS

*There Is Only Plan A*

Copyright © 2014 Klay S. Williams

All Rights Reserved

KLAY SILAS WILLIAMS is the co-owner of Harrison Williams, a lifestyle consulting firm based in New York City. Born and raised in Detroit, Michigan, Klay is a graduate of Kalamazoo College, where he earned a Bachelor of Arts degree in Religion with a double minor in Economics and Business. He holds a Master of Divinity degree from Princeton Theological Seminary.

Through his leadership and philosophy of *There Is Only Plan A*, Klay has unlocked a singular powerhouse where individuals can learn how to live their complete and best life.

Edited by Darcy Quigley

Cover design by Hal Sadler

*For My Plan A Friends*

The

    **Journey**

        Is

            Always

                Perfect

# TABLE OF CONTENTS

INTRODUCTION ..................................................................... 1

PLAN A, PART I: GOD ........................................................... 7
    Chapter 1: I Want to Believe ............................................... 9
    Chapter 2: The Ralph Lauren Experience ....................... 15
    Chapter 3: Let Me Be Your Angel ..................................... 21

PLAN A, PART II: VISION .................................................... 27
    Chapter 4: Let the Moment Live In You ........................... 29

PLAN A, PART III: BELIEF ................................................... 33
    Chapter 5: Do You Hear the Music? .................................. 35

PLAN A, PART IV: HARD WORK ..................................... 41
    Chapter 6: The Waiting Game ........................................... 43
    Chapter 7: Somewhere Over the Perseverance Rainbow ............. 49
    Chapter 8: Plan A Friendships .......................................... 55
    Chapter 9: Pardon Me ....................................................... 63
    Chapter 10: Down With the King ..................................... 69
    Chapter 11: It's Never Too Much ...................................... 75
    Chapter 12: Thank You. More Please. ............................... 81

**PLAN A, PART V: SURRENDER** ............................................. 85

    Chapter 13: I Surrender All ............................................. 87

**CONCLUSION** ............................................................................. 93

    Chapter 14: I'm Coming Home ....................................... 95

**APPENDIX: PLAN A APHORISMS** ........................... 101

# ACKNOWLEDGEMENTS

I stand in amazement, gratitude, and honor to have experienced such a level of unwavering support from incredible Plan A friends and family around the world. Your generous hearts of kindness, encouragement, and authenticity have paved a way for Plan A to live and thrive. While your names are too many to mention, please know that I am eternally grateful for each of you. Thank you! Thank you! Thank you!

To my editor, Darcy Quigley, as I have said in countless conversations with you, this book would not be possible without your gifts and talents. Thank you for your honesty, dedication, and commitment in seeing this project through to the end. Our united journey has allowed me to grow in a manner that I once could only hope for, but now experience.

To my graphic designer, Hal Sadler, thank you so very much for allowing me to experience comic relief beyond comprehension, amazing graphic design, and guidance.

Mom, thank you for nurturing my gifts at a very early age and forcing me to dream, prepare, and understand my worth. You're a remarkable woman whose strength and determination could never be expressed through words—just in heart. I heart you.

Dad, as a child I never quite understood your love of teachers such as Dr. Wayne W. Dyer and Joyce Meyer. Now I do. Thank you for paving the way in teaching me how to understand God and humanity in a different context.

A very special thank you to my best friend and sister, Kathryn. I never had to go out and search for friendship, because I've always had you to show me what the gift of friendship truly means.

And to my brother, Kenneth, thank you for always being a grounding force that reminds me to remember faith and purpose.

Friends, there were many times that I could not see a way forward, but each of you carried my dream until I could find strength again. The baton of faith traveled to each of your homes, hearts, and spirits. I only hope and dream that I can be the friend that each of you has been to me.

**Dear God,**

*I had a great day today for several reasons—or actually a bittersweet day. I took my sister Kathy to the airport and I almost became teary-eyed, because I'm going to miss her. The transitional period is a very complex situation. Of course you have 'desire' and 'fear' running neck and neck. While both emotions are important in order for one to gain wisdom, both emotions cannot equally coexist in our world of peace. Therefore, I choose 'desire.' I choose 'passion.' I choose 'freedom.' I choose 'truth.' And most of all, I choose 'the promise of God.' A lot of things are becoming revealed as I take the initiative to embark upon this bold direction. Not only am I interested in succeeding, I'm interested in internal success that says, "I am happy and joyous in the world; the work that I do is meaningful." I now connect with God, my gifts and talents that I've been blessed with…I've decided to take risks and experience all that life has to offer. Let the moment live in you! God now draws closer to me as my eyes, heart, and emotions are opened to new senses. I feel this presence ever near to me and ask God to remain at the center of my heart. God lives within me and I am a part of the flow of life. I am blessed beyond my dreams and gifted; I now choose to rise to my God-given potential and take New York and the world by storm. My arms are open wide and ready to embrace all joys, yet diverse trials might surface…*

# INTRODUCTION

*Aren't you tired of being someone that you're clearly not? "But the road to success is..." is what you've been telling yourself. No, the road to success is governed and "sustained" by those who are authentically themselves. Give it a try and watch unopened doors suddenly appear to be available in every direction you turn. Dare to not be 'ordinary.'*

I had no idea that dying a spiritual death could be so liberating. The idea that I could begin a new life, with new forms of consciousness and a new pathway, governed by purpose and calling, has completely altered life for me. Am I really supposed to feel so authentically present, courageous, and powerful? My mind and body seemed to have longed for this soul transformation to occur years ago. I guess it's never too late to respond to this notion of calling and purpose. The only form of regret would be to not seek out our individual meanings in life and deny ourselves the ability to thrive at our very best.

As children, we were asked, "Who do you want to be when you grow up?" This question conjures up monumental abstracts of people fulfilling wonderful posts in the world without an eraser to correct our explosive dreams. Today, as adults, we stop asking ourselves this question and transition into a life that is safe, predictable, and monotonous, lacking substance even on our best day. Because we are still "growing" as individuals, self-discovery of one's Plan A is not restricted to our 20s, 30s, 40s, or 50s. However, the importance of this journey lies in the realization that Plan A must take place in order for us to truly experience life. Plan

A does not discriminate against age disparities, but does discriminate against inefficient levels of existing. We will never miss our window of opportunity to function at the highest level of our capabilities, as long as we seek out the universal plan that is our individual mission in the world. Ask, receive, and begin in yourself an undeniable path of work that will stretch you beyond your understanding—a movement that will utilize every untapped gift inside of you that you've always fantasized expressing, giving you the courage to move beyond structures that have paralyzed your ability to act and a spiritual journey that will invite you to live again.

Plan A is the discovery, recognition, and acceptance of one's calling and purpose in life. It's the sustaining measures of the journey that you will embark upon in hopes of conquering your dream. It's the lived experience and specialness that are your task and mission while here on earth. While the stories, thoughts, and explanations that you will bear witness to are a part of my personal experience, it is my belief that there is a universal experience that is common when seeking to obtain your own Plan A. The philosophy of Plan A operates under a specific formula, which serves as a pilot for guidance, realization, cultivation, lived experience, and release.

# PLAN A FORMULA

### God

*We ask how we may be of service to God/the Universe and humanity*

### Vision

*God then gives us a vision or discovery of our Plan A*

### Belief

*It is then imperative that we offer the vibration of belief and faith to support our Plan A*

### Hard Work

*Perseverance and hard work then carry us through the often-tumultuous journey of resistance toward fulfilling our Plan A*

### Surrender

*After doing everything humanly possible to accomplish our goal, we must surrender our dream and trust in a higher power to realize our Plan A*

Plan A simply asks the question, "Does my life reflect who I was called to be?" from an interior and exterior point of reference. Am I offering my very best person to the world, to my area of work, and—most importantly—to myself? There is an unexplainable feeling that you will experience by submitting to the energy that the Universe offers. Perfection is not required in order to live a life powered by Plan A. The only requirement of Plan A is complete trust in an unfamiliar route you may never have traveled before, but wholly believe in. After discovering your Plan A, life will appear to start again. New senses will arise and different states of being will exist. You will look back at your old life and wonder, "Who in the world was that?"

And this is what this journey is all about—being thankful for who you were and now ready to embrace who you were born to be.

The rewards of living, being, and responding to Plan A are immeasurable and limitless beyond our scope of imagination. However, I must stress that this journey is **not** an easy process at all. Before you purchase this book and decide to venture down the road to ultimate sustainable success, ask yourself if you're ready and willing to do the work necessary to fulfill your Plan A. While book sales revenue has its place in sustaining me as a writer, I'm more concerned with your willingness to authentically travel this voyage with me and not allow this book to collect dust on your shelf. The transformation that you will experience through my journey may serve as a catalyst for you to have courage and faith to begin your own personal journey. Nonetheless, this book will not perform the work for you. The process of fulfilling your Plan As starts with your individual self and requires you to be open and agreeable to the path that will unavoidably present itself before you. The mere fact that you selected this book to read in this precise moment is vital in one way or another in your life. However, be honest with yourself and search your heart for where you are and the level of commitment that you are ready to exercise.

Unbeknownst to us, Plan A has always been working in our lives, but has required us to recognize its call, understand its meaning, and make peace with the gift that is bestowed to each of us. Understanding our Plan As might come to us through unconventional mediums, as you

## INTRODUCTION

will discover through my experience. However, sometimes the key that unlocks a world of difference and meaning could literally be right in front of us, but goes without acknowledgment. There are no coincidences in life, and as soon as we acknowledge this understanding, the more alert our senses will become and the more we will take advantage of being present in the moment. The call of Plan A would be easier for us to recognize and obtain if we give ourselves permission to slow down and take each second, minute, and hour as a precious gift. Our lives will become more defined and we will no longer dance in the waves of life by ourselves; we will receive a partner who will confidently take our hand—leading and guiding, until it's our turn to make the next move.

Responding to our Plan As is the greatest gift of gratitude we could give to God, the Universe for giving us life and unique special talents. Not acting upon our individual modes of purpose inevitably robs the world of the natural progression towards a balanced level of enlightenment, peace, and collective harmony. Imagine if every person that you communicated with in your daily life operated from a place of wholeness, authenticity, and in alignment with his or her Plan A. The universal impact would be greater than we could ever envision. Love in all forms could rule our interactions and rid the planet of deceit, greed, and practices of evil. The axis of our world would rotate upon happiness, while all levels of fear would cease to exist. Plan A means that we recognize the infinite power that resides in us and acknowledge the Spirit that is at work at our center. This Spirit will be the governing force with which we can meditate and whose infinite wisdom we can seek out. In turn, the Spirit asks us to then share our wisdom and lived experience with others.

Plan A will refresh your life button and allow you to use your creative imagination once again. Have you not missed using your imagination? Have you been so engulfed with dismay and fruitless in your pessimistic world of thinking that you've denied any possibility of change to surface? Here's an opportunity to terminate old methods of existence and a chance to reshape your life once again.

It is my hope that you will listen to the voice that is present in each of the chapters of this book, and will seek to find your own voice. The voice of hope, change, persistence, and faith does exist and you will find it at the heart of Plan A. There's only Plan A and, because there is only Plan A, there is no reason why your God-given dream cannot come true.

And so it begins…

# PLAN A, PART I: GOD

*We ask how we may be of service to God,
the Universe, and humanity*

*Dear God,*

*I am in a state of questioning, pondering, delivering, and creativity, and in a medium of action. I am leaving the mission agency. I have asked God, the Universe to come to my aid, that my soul is dying and I have not heard much at all from that Power…maybe I need to look within…but God, where are you? I need to find purpose, love, and financial growth within my craft…the gifts that I've been given…I have responded to my calling…but nothing. Nothing. Nothing. I still have hope. My stride still struts to its somewhat damaged walk…I'm still a star. I'm a world changer. I am a lifestylist. I am…I am…I am. It's hard at times, this idea of being special, this idea of calling. I wonder what life would be like if I just went to Corporate America in some fashion? I may. I need a break. I am trying. The artist in me is in need of the creative master to work in my favor…to help me help myself. God, please send help.*

# CHAPTER 1:
# I WANT TO BELIEVE

*It's never my job to tell people what they should or should not believe in, but having faith in something beside ourselves makes life a tad bit easier.*

Over the years, my understanding regarding faith, acts of grace, mercy, miracles, and experiences with the supernatural has caused me to pause and reflect upon the foundation for my beliefs. Is there a God that is in control of our experiences? Of our destiny? Do my spiritual beliefs coincide with the manner in which I live my life—or is it a form of conditioning that was passed down within my family lineage? What is it that I believe? And if I do have belief in something "greater" than myself, what evidence supports my claim—for me?

As a child growing up in a religious family, I often found myself at various spiritual events that took place at our church and shared in the customs that would shape my existence. For a lot of us who are in the process of discovering and/or naming what deity to follow or spiritual principles to subscribe to, there is a fear of becoming a follower of one specific religion. What if you could be Christian and follow aspects of Buddhism or Zoroastrianism? What if you were a Muslim and subscribed to certain principles of Judaism? What if you did not care to name a specific deity from any particular religion, but simply believed in a universal God and the principles of goodness, faithfulness, and love of humanity? As farfetched as some of the above ideas might be, we are living in a world where people believe in something higher than themselves, but are afraid to actually voice their spiritual conviction because it does not follow a precise doctrinal path. In most conversations I have on this topic, the ultimate fear I encounter is, "Is it okay for me to question if there's a God?" I would have to answer, "Yes."

Plan A recognizes the limitless resource that is God, functioning as the co-Creator of our destiny. However, Plan A does not force anyone to follow a particular trek without questioning the validity of one's faith, a supernatural being, and universal aid. I've come to realize that the spiritual component of Plan A is something that works for me and clients that have a shared desire to wrestle with life's meanings. These are individuals who ultimately want to live a complete and best life, but lack skills and a safe environment to authentically have a spiritually enlightened experience. The practices highlighted within Plan A have tremendously aided me in my life, increased my faith in God, and provided me with unlimited hope. I think it's okay to say that you're on a spiritual journey to better understand who you are and your potential relationship to something greater than yourself.

Nonetheless, Plan A first suggests that everyone has a task and/or mission to perform while here on earth. The Universe has charged each person with a monumental job, regardless of how big or small we personally view its function to be. I believe that if we really want to better understand who we are, what area of life to follow or how to further develop our personhood, the answer begins with the questions, "God, how can I be of service to you and the world? What task(s) do you ask of me to perform?" Plan A suggests that once we have an understanding and connection with God, there is a heightened level of connection to the Universe at large. Life occurrences will not only direct us within our purpose, but our relationships to all things on earth will be strengthened, challenged, and changed for our best good. Opening ourselves to receive our purpose and calling gives us a better quality of life, but also wages extreme responsibility. Therefore, the vignettes depicted within this book do not reflect a hypothetical situation, but a true reality. When we begin to respond to our Plan A in life, opposition sets in and the opportunity to grow and be strengthened is exerted. It's very important

## CHAPTER 1: I WANT TO BELIEVE

to allow ourselves the chance to experience the various levels of resistance that will inevitably come our way, because the lessons, experiences, and understandings will prepare us for the tasks at hand. It's a spiritually grounding experience that will certainly strengthen one's walk with God.

Second, the spiritual path of Plan A recognizes that God does not place us in any happenstance situations that are not a part of our Plan A. The trick is not to look at an experience as a waste of time, but as a chance to receive bonus insights that will have an impact on our destined state. Several experiences in my life have caused me to pause and ask, "God, where are you? Why are you allowing these bad things to happen to me?" After listing a litany of good qualities that I possess and performing a comparison of my life to other people who supposedly "Never experience grief," I slowly gained insight that would change my method of thinking. As a result of our individualized paths, there are things that we will go through in life that function as a form of conditioning and are unique to our experience. God does not choose to harm us or allow painful things to happen. Nonetheless, God asks if we will trust and allow ourselves an opportunity to believe in a presence that will propel us to a greater cause and sense of self. However, as my good friend Rachel Harvey says, "It's not about asking 'Where is God?' The appropriate question is, 'Where are you?'"

I think of my life trajectory of trying to understand the faithfulness and partnered goodness that I have felt submitting my life to God. When I became an employee at the global-based mission agency, I had no idea why I was there and how this would help me with my Plan A. Although this form of serving humanity and the Universe was a great opportunity, I thought that it did not have any direct bearing on my personal Plan A. I already understood what I was suppose to do on earth, but could not understand through my limited knowledge the importance of this experience. After submitting my letter of resignation to the nonprofit organization, several coworkers approached me and inquired about my next opportunity. Normally, I would sluggishly volunteer such information, but I felt compelled to share. Before I could finish the concept of revamping the company that I would soon restart, a graphic designer stated, "Oh, you need new business cards, stationery, note cards, and a logo. I'll design all of these things for free!" I then hear the production coordinator offer, "Oh, great! I'll call our vendors and get the best quality stock paper at virtually no cost to you!" And running around the corner is an editor who states, "This is great! I will edit your documents for you…and wait, do I hear that you're also writing a book?" I would then ask her to edit this book! I also gained a spiritual mentor through this experience and lifelong friends who are constant supportive aides as I move through my own Plan A journey. This was nothing but the Universe acting as the ultimate provisional aid, allowing every experience of uncertainty, fear, defeat, and hurt to transition into a state of inexorable opportunity.

God is the force of goodness that is a never-ending stream of beginnings and a knowledge that will always circumvent our mental capacities. While we have the ability to dream, feel, and exert a spectacular idea of Plan A, God is the force behind our purpose and will only amplify our Plan A beyond comprehension. Utilizing our internal guide, acts of goodness, and mental capacity to dream is a part of conquering our Plan A, but through the use of recognizing and utilizing the power that is God, our dreams are magnified to a level that we will never be able to conquer on our own. And in my personal faith journey, I've discovered that this unlimited source is available to anyone who would allow oneself an opportunity to believe.

Third, we might wonder to ourselves, "How do I know that God is here with me, through the good and bad times?" When experiencing highs and lows of Plan A, God is a multidimensional power that functions as a comforter, encourager, healer, proud parent, and source of joy throughout our journey. The mechanism of gratitude that one experiences when a discovery of true purpose is received, the first client is booked, or a newly leased office for a company start has begun, is a feeling of indescribable sensation that is difficult to explain to others. There is an internal knowing that is applied and a speechless form of triumph that is felt, and this is God. God is the unspeakable joy that overshadows our knowledge or understanding. Have you ever felt this presence? If not, examine your life journey to your Plan A closely and ask yourself, "Is this

## CHAPTER 1: I WANT TO BELIEVE

a journey that I can afford to travel on my own?" When experiencing the difficult modes of resistance within our Plan A journey, there are times when we may feel that we should quit, abandon our dream, or travel a path that is easier. This is a human feeling that usually comes with the experience. Nonetheless, the God experience is the force that allows us to have our moment, but ultimately tells us to stop feeling sorry for ourselves, to trust our intuition, and is the aide that picks us up from the ground, thrusting us back to the course towards our Plan A.

There are various forms of exercising faith and spirituality in the world. I often hear individuals from diverse cultural backgrounds explain their spiritual values and beliefs, but they are confused as to what principle doctrinal faith to follow. I answer with…follow God. Love, justice, mercy, forgiveness, faithfulness, surrender, giving, kindness, perseverance, and various other attributes of true goodness are all God. Ask the power of all power to be your guide and move you towards the spiritual place that is your sustaining force. My life is powered by Plan A and for me, Plan A is powered by a deity that protects, loves, challenges, forgives, and provides rest. Plan A is not a journey of faith comparisons, but a journey that asks us to serve and believe, and eventually have the courage to rise to our God-given potential.

***Dear God,***

*Wow, is it too good to be true? Am I almost there? The general manager from Ralph Lauren Short Hills called me yesterday and told me that he wants me for the job! My hope is not really hope but realization, rather that the Universe always provides, as long as we remain faithful and steadfast. I mean, I prayed and asked for a positive change this summer, a change for renewal, and it appears that the right steps are being taken. I realize more and more that I am here for helping people. My good friend always tells me that leaders are sometimes born, made, and created with time. This summer is one of peace, happiness, growth, new experiences, excitement, and fun. I hope to be the person that God has called me to become…*

# CHAPTER 2:
# THE RALPH LAUREN EXPERIENCE

*I am always at the right place, at the right time.*

As The Oprah Winfrey Show has come to an end, in Oprah's final season, viewers worldwide were fascinated by the awe-inspiring home, lifestyle, and family that were showcased—the family of fashion designer Ralph Lauren. Mr. Lauren and Oprah surveyed his beautiful home, located in the Rocky Mountains, called, the "RRL" Ranch, where picturesque visions of fascinating eclectic and luxury décor, beautiful elongated wooden fences, and detailed rooms filled the immense space. Immediately, I was taken back to the first time that I met Mr. Lauren, at the Ralph Lauren Sports Store in New York City.

While attending Princeton Theological Seminary for grad school, I decided to take a job at Banana Republic in Palmer Square, a beautiful oasis of specialty shops, restaurants, and boutiques located in the center of Princeton's downtown. While working as a sales associate for three weeks, a very interesting woman approached me, inquiring about a sweater she saw on a mannequin. After answering her question, she complimented me on my smile and insisted that I did not belong at BR, but elsewhere—across the street at a store that would be opening soon—Polo Ralph Lauren. After a round of exciting interviews, I decided that I would take the job.

Shortly after beginning work at Ralph Lauren, it was decided that our staff would be rigged in RL clothing as a gift, to celebrate the opening of the new store. As I entered the walls of what would soon be my spiritual haven, a discreet, intriguing, and charismatic man surfaced from behind a display of perfectly placed cashmere sweaters. It was Mr. Lauren. After introducing myself, he asked me a couple of questions regarding the new store and whether I was happy and excited, and then he offered advice in terms of what I could do to be my best self in the RL environment. He was calm, peaceful, and made me feel that I was the only individual in the room.

Many people who teeter between understanding the need for luxury and lifestyle or viewing it as just overpriced clothing might not understand the vision that is behind Ralph Lauren's kingdom. The one word that defines the Ralph Lauren Experience versus other high-fashion empires is: Love. Ralph Lauren has created a dynasty of specialty items that is about accomplishing one's best inner self in almost every area of human engagement, via the art form of living. As he suggests, "I'm not about fashion, I'm about living." I translate this understanding into components of what Plan A means. Plan A, in this instance, might be misunderstood as a desire for expensive things. More accurately, Plan A is the desire to be your very best in whatever regard gives you an arena for extreme self-expression; it is the place where peace, reality, and spirit are met and you gain the fortitude of understanding that you are becoming closer and closer to your center. No wonder I was able to experience one of the most profound spiritual expressions of my life at Polo Ralph Lauren.

While across the street I was obtaining a Master of Divinity degree at Princeton, I was amazed by the level of creative expression, inner peace, and opportunity to find "the Sacred" that I discovered working at Ralph Lauren. Ironically, my proposed Plan A mission of being a pastor evolved and transformed into going beyond the confines of traditional forms of ministry—combining my love for helping to guide individuals to find passageways and mechanisms to fulfill their life's purpose, dreams, and heart's longing, with that of fashion—and thus was born Plan A.

## CHAPTER 2: THE RALPH LAUREN EXPERIENCE

As an insider who walked the hallowed halls of Polo Ralph Lauren, I was able to realize firsthand the jubilation, transformation, and self-expression experienced by most clients who graced our presence. The Ralph Lauren experience is about more than selling clothing; it's about connecting on a human, creative, and spiritual level with everyday people—giving them a moment to remember how special they are, under a guise of detailed, elegant garments.

While rigging clients in the most imaginative and exceptional frocks, I discovered that another level needed to be enhanced for the full experience of what I understood to be the essence of Mr. Lauren—which I would also need for my own personal development. I began teaching clients how to delve beneath the layer of each garment and connect the beautiful person they would see on the outside, with the one they would like to become on the inside. Before I knew it, clients insisted on having me over for dinner, lunch, or drinks to talk about their quality of life. The more I began to look beyond the confined box of what I viewed as ministry, the more I became alive, present, and able to connect my center with that of the Divine. I felt a connection that I had never experienced before, an opportunity to move outside of myself and release my true spirit—almost in a sense of being born again.

I like to think that when we are first born, there is of course a sense of purity and freedom that is met with every baby. I also think that this is the only time for most human beings that they can and will ever be their true authentic selves. At this stage, life's web of control and inflicted 'isms' of who we should or should not be have not yet overtaken the soul; we're rendered perfect, whole, and courageous. However, within this given experience at Polo Ralph Lauren, I was born again—because I discovered my true life's purpose and calling. In hindsight, a glimpse of what I would call my Plan A was revealed to me in this moment.

The Ralph Lauren experience gave me an opportunity to further hone my creative skills and increase my spiritual faith in the universe. Yes, I agree that experiences such as these are available to us everywhere, but I also believe that because of who Ralph Lauren is and the spirit that he emits, there is an interconnectivity that is transmitted to his designs, homes, and most importantly, the staff that works for him.

One day, very soon, I will meet with him again and offer my thanks for unknowingly pushing me to be my best self through this experience. He gave me permission to work toward my Plan A. In turn, it has petitioned me to do the same for others.

***Dear God,***

*Class, class, wonderful class. Forty-seven days to go until my career at Princeton is over, give or take; I am sort of sitting on the edge of a possible new career or just a fresh start. I have two interviews tomorrow that will probably finalize my time and/or experience for the next couple of years. I'm searching for a new home, for happiness, joy, a career, a time to actually have a chance to enjoy life, and see what the world has to offer. Every place and experience comes with a change; it is my hope that change will be positive. I mean, who knows what new life is ahead for me? I'm not sure. I feel as though remaining steadfast in God, true to myself, remembering my parents' morals and values that they've instilled in me is what I'll have to take. I decided a while ago to live my life for me and explore the things that I desire...*

# CHAPTER 3:
# LET ME BE YOUR ANGEL

*I was greeted this morning with the most amazing sunshine, a torrential outpouring of joy spilling over from my soul, and a message from the universe kindly whispering, "Let me be your angel…." And I gladly accepted its request.*

For many of us who are trying to understand and gain a full picture of what our Plan A looks like, we realize that not knowing can be a very painful experience. How many times are you at a party or a celebration for a friend who just graduated with a specialized degree in a particular field, and the individual not only understands what his/her Plan A looks like but has also begun the process? Or you've just celebrated with a good friend who hosted a party to launch his/her new clothing store, legal practice, or culinary business, and you're left wondering, "When am I going to find my Plan A? How many more events will I go to and cheer on others, when I am pleading with the world to just give me a glimpse, if not an answer to what my Plan A is all about?" As the accumulation of each of these celebrations and discoveries from close friends—or distant 'star-friends' we've adopted on television—becomes too much for us to handle, there comes a breaking point of frustration, depression, and anger with the world. This leaves me with a burning question that I must ask: Are you sure that you did not receive a "green flag" with an answer to your question?

We have become accustomed to hearing the expression, "red flag," but may not be familiar with "green flags." When we hear the term "red flag," we automatically think of a message from the universe giving us a sign that we should not go in a certain direction, whether it's a budding romantic relationship, business opportunity, or other engagements of our choosing. Whether we opt to ignore or accept the red flag that is always given to us will determine the next direction our lives will take. Often, after we have found acceptance in red flag/hazardous situations, we may say to close friends, or ourselves, "Something was protecting me from this situation. I'm so glad that I heeded the red flag." I believe that this "something" is a higher power that allows us to determine our very own path, but acts as a guiding force. It's as if you're kayaking down a river, and at first the water seems to be somewhat calm. Then suddenly the water becomes tumultuous, swaying you in various directions. You become panicked and scared. Out of nowhere a strong wind from the east comes and gives you and your kayak enough force to guide you to shore. As soon as you reach the land, you may say, "I'm not sure how I survived, but thank God I did." This same guiding force is telling us, "Let me be your angel," and not only gives us red flags as signs of caution or "do not enter" but also gives us green flags that say, "Go." Confusing? Let me explain.

Just as we always receive a red flag in regards to a negative occurrence that could potentially harm us, we also always receive a green flag for a positive occurrence. However, just as we often do with a negative red flag, we tend to ignore the positive green flag that is attempting to give us a glimpse of our Plan A.

A month or so after my graduation from Princeton, I moved home to Michigan to figure out the next steps of my Plan A. I did not know exactly what I wanted to do—how I could utilize my passion for helping better the human condition with that of nurturing my artistic desires. I just knew that I did not want to return to retail management. While the fashion world greatly intrigued me, there was something more that my soul craved. I didn't quite understand why I had not received an omen or sign of what was next. After all, I was about to graduate from seminary! Wasn't I supposed to know what the universe had called me to?

## CHAPTER 3: LET ME BE YOUR ANGEL

This perplexing thought plagued me for quite some time. I finished final papers a month before classes ended for graduating students. I did all of the 'right' things (sound familiar?), and had additional time to focus on finding my next placement. I was offered a wonderful position at the flagship store of Tom Ford before its scheduled spring opening. Before going into my last meeting to accept or decline the position, I questioned the base salary that was offered, but that was not the real matter of concern.

A day prior to my meeting, I was visiting with a good friend who was helping me decipher the pros and cons of accepting the offer. At the end of the conversation, I concluded that this would be a great opportunity as a filler job, but I was not entirely sold on accepting the position. A very small window of uncertainty continued to whisper, "This is not where your heart completely lies. Stop fretting the next steps and trust." My friend excused herself to the next room and on her couch was a book entitled, *You Can Heal Your Life* by Louise Haye. I thought the title was very interesting and opened the book to a random page and read the following phrase: "I trust the process of life to bring me my highest good."[1] My positive green flag had come.

I reflected on the green flag and respectfully declined the position. While working for such an amazing fashion empire would have been an incredible experience, it was not where I was supposed to be. Nevertheless, I think that my green flag gave me a glimpse of knowing that fashion would be a part of my Plan A. While I did not know the entire picture, I received a small preview of my Plan A, and I believed that I could move on and trust life. It was enough for the moment, and that was all that I could really ask from the Universe, as I was left with a sensation of peace.

I learned that in the same way that a red flag protects us from an experience, green flags give us passageways to our Plan As, if only we open our hearts to their calling. Regardless of how subtly or quietly our positive green flags appear, they are always there. Nonetheless, most of us discover the track records of green flags given to us only after we've reached

---

[1] Louise L. Hay, *You Can Heal Your Life* (Hay House, Inc., 1999), 104.

our destination. I wonder what would really happen if we allowed ourselves the opportunity to see the positive within what we deem to be negative? I think that if we conditioned ourselves to wait for what could be a small or large window of opportunity, we could potentially achieve mastery of patience, the ability to learn from a negative situation, and a chance to open our minds to witness green flags, however they manifest in our lives.

After declining this job opportunity and returning to Michigan for a reprieve, I discovered that I would need to create something that could utilize both my theological training and my creative pursuits, but what? This was the part of my journey where exercising stillness would have been beneficial in further discovering my Plan A. Unfortunately, I did not possess the patience or the will, at the time, to allow the Universe to be my angel. I complained, was depressed for the entire summer, and was virtually a monster to my family. Interestingly enough, there were several positive green flags that appeared—encouraging me to write out what I wanted to do—via friends, television commercials, random emails from former clients, and other thought-provoking mediums. The 'how' would construct itself, but I rejected that notion.

Close to the end of the summer I received a call from my previous manager at Ralph Lauren. He was one of the best supervisors, mentors, and friends I ever had, and he would check in with me from time to time. He had recently matriculated to another luxury brand company and was searching for an assistant general manager. My friend offered me the position and I immediately accepted without giving it much thought. I packed my car up the next week and drove back east to begin my new life.

As I walked into the store, I was extremely happy to see my boss. We exchanged greetings as I toured the store. However, within a few minutes, my emotional state would change. "Oh, no!" I thought to myself. A feeling of utter claustrophobia, injury and coldness came over me. For the remainder of the day, I had no idea what was occurring, but needed to sort it out that night.

## CHAPTER 3: LET ME BE YOUR ANGEL

At the end of the day I talked with my boss, as he could tell that something was wrong. He was very encouraging and asked me to go home, get a good night's rest, and start fresh the next day. I stayed up all that night trying to work through this issue. I panicked and cried throughout the night, because I knew that I was not where I was suppose to be. Why did I not listen to my angel? Why did I ignore the green flags that were manifesting in my life? What should I do now? Quit? If I quit, what would happen to my boss? Our friendship? His trust in me? I was in a very precarious situation. I started fumbling through my bag and pulled out a copy of a new book I had started to read, *The Invitation* by Oriah. I came to a very difficult conclusion as I read: "…it doesn't interest me if the story you are telling me is true. I want to know if you can disappoint another to be true to yourself."[2] Silence and embarrassing truth came over me.

The next morning I phoned my boss and returned the advance relocation check I had received. The disappointment in his voice was enough to haunt my heart for quite some time. I packed my car yet again, and returned to Michigan, this time if only to listen to the positive green flags and allow the universe to be my guiding force—a major part of living out our Plan A. Had I listened to what the Universe was trying to communicate to me the first time, maybe a friendship could have been salvaged. But if I hadn't followed that inner voice the second time around, I'm not sure where I might be today.

It is not a good idea to be reckless with our decision-making or to blatantly betray a friend or confidant. It is important to allow ourselves the opportunity to be still long enough for the process of life to take place. Sometimes our human time clock impedes our ability to be centered within the Universe's time frame. Unknowingly, through our impatience, we get in our own way in the pursuit of our Plan A. The universe acts as a governing force that protects and propels us toward our end goal, if only we allow its loving hand to guide us toward our next destination.

---

2   Oriah, *The Invitation* (HarperCollins, 2006), 57.

# PLAN A, PART II: VISION

*God then gives us a vision or discovery of our Plan A*

***Dear God,***

*Some people say dreams never come true. Others believe that they only come true if you're lucky, while several individuals believe that dreams are some sort of mystical wonder. I don't know if dreams are miracles or things that one has motivation, inspiration, or simply hope in, but they do come true...*

# CHAPTER 4:
# LET THE MOMENT LIVE IN YOU

*"Oh, they're just so lucky," we say to ourselves as we watch friends or total strangers in careers that we want, living a life that we long to live, and creatively expressing new ideas and thoughts. "Why them? Why not me? I work hard!" you might say to yourself. Well, the only course of action that is different is that they 'believe' in their dream and you do not. Dreams without true belief are empty and cannot come to fruition.*

The past several years have awakened a universal nervous energy inside most of us who are in search of a magic remedy, vaccine, or antibiotic that would give back our sense of self-worth—something that could cure our inability to be present and renew our aptitude to be the co-Creator of our own destiny. With financial recession, job loss, natural disasters, and other difficult measures at an all-time high, a lot of us are seeking out measures and mechanisms to create new lives for ourselves. We have exhausted all potential ideas within our own level of resources and have followed advice from others and nothing new, exciting, or innovative has come from our work.

While life has a way of bamboozling our state of mind into creating a defeatist attitude or point of view that renders us powerless, that same mechanism can also generate a powerful frequency of optimism. This is lived out in our minds when we first form a concept—that is, an idea or notion (whether positive or negative). Therefore, that which we have mentally created is that which 'shall be.' If we say to ourselves, "I will never have enough money to buy this home," or, "I'll never find the man or woman of my dreams," or, "I would love to go after a promotion, but I don't think I will get the job," then we never will. It's just as simple as that.

Think of it this way: if negativity, depression, and fear have ruled your thought process, bringing you continuous streams of nothingness, what do you have to lose by giving a new process a chance? We are screaming to the world, "Increase! Increase! Enlarge my territory!" with empty hearts of true disbelief, words that are simply void at our very core—as if we can fool the universe into pouring out a manifestation of gifts that we do not entirely believe in.

Creating visions through your mind and seeing yourself in the reality that you desire is not enough to conquer your Plan A. It's not enough to place you in the CEO chair, not enough to become an Olympic gold medalist in the 1,500 meter free swim, and not enough for you to declare candidacy for President of the United States of America. Visioning must turn into believing. Plan A says that you must believe in your ability to be that which the universe has called you to be—knowing that you may not have the skills to land your dream job in the immediacy, but trusting that the 'how' of your destiny is already managed by the Higher Power. You manifest that trust by being present in the moment, offering gratitude to the heavens for where you are in life at this present time, and living into the role of that which you are aspiring to become in the moment. This means that if your desire is to be the Head Diversity Recruiter of a law firm, you will begin to look the part in this present moment (more on this later), and step out of your comfort zone to network with the very best in the industry. If I aspire to be a philanthropist, I will begin to develop a cause and introduce myself as: Klay S. Williams, Philanthropist. Remember, the 'how' of it is not your concern. This is the job of your divine partner, the co-Creator of your destiny. Plan A says that our job is to search our hearts and minds for authentic aspirations, goals, and dreams that we have been afraid to voice out loud.

## CHAPTER 4: LET THE MOMENT LIVE IN YOU

Plan A visioning is not a method of magical sorcery or the ability to pull a rabbit from a magician's hat. Visioning is releasing all that you desire and feel called to be through a method of connecting your co-Creator (God), present circumstance, and future journey into a juxtaposition of communal reality—as in not only visualizing your special path but also actually seeing yourself accomplishing your goal. It's a process that requires vulnerability of self, alignment with your co-Creator, and the courage to ask yourself difficult questions, such as: *What is holding me back from living out my "Plan A"? What is my contribution to the world? What are my fears? What are my gifts? Do I truly believe that I am deserving? What are my insecurities? Do I love myself? Will I upset family, friends, and society if I choose to be someone different than who they think I am or want me to be? Who am I, really?* These are all questions that will be important as we seek to discover our "Plan A"s together.

After answering some of these very difficult questions (and others), you'll begin to see a path that is yours and yours alone. This is called your "Plan A." Allowing yourself the opportunity to dream gives you the chance to discover your Plan A. The Universe is in the midst of your dreaming process and will help guide you to your Plan A as you seek out God's will for your life. We will discover this more as the book progresses.

Develop your Plan A by creating a vision board of everything that is in your heart, in whatever creative method captures your attention and maintains your focus. A vision board can include words, photos, drawings, cutouts, or any form that you desire, contained in a centralized location that you're able to see every day. Vision boards help serve as a physical manifestation of your Plan A that you are seeking to accomplish. In an uncanny yet artistic method, it helps ease your mind and almost gives you an added benefit of assurance that you can accomplish your end goal. Your willingness to boldly place your dreams on paper will center your heart and mind on actually releasing the feeling that your Plan A is already accomplished. Some of us may have wonderful levels of imagination, but taking our time to create such gifts in physical form helps prepare us for the journey that we will begin. In times of despair and uncertainty, vision boards allow you to refocus on the end result and remember the energy and feeling you felt when you projected your goals out into the world. Therefore, the 'moments' of life that you are seeking to accomplish do not become a lofty and impossible goal—the moment that you are seeking to obtain will always live in you. You are not then seeking to reach for a special moment to occur, but it (your Plan A manifestation) has already occurred. If you allow yourselves to visualize and place authentic belief behind your end goal, life will do the rest. Visualization then helps form in you a mode of acceptance that your Plan A is here, dwelling with and within you. Remember, directions and paths change all the time, so do not feel as though you cannot create a vision board if you're uneasy about your life's dreams changing.

Walk your way out of this mentality of recession and depression into a mode of visualization and manifestation. Now is your time. Not because I say so, but because you believe it to be so! Utilize and share with the world all of the beautiful gifts that are waiting to be tapped inside of you. Become victorious in your own right to be the successful individual that you have always been destined to become. Have a moment of disappointment when life goes in a direction that is not on your wavelength. Bumps and bruises in life will come, as that is a part of the universal experience. It's not the situation that will determine your future, but how you respond to the situation. Visualization is a beginning for you to speak life into your circumstance and not fear. Once you accomplish your Plan A, you will notice that everything that you always needed was living within you from the very beginning. The only response that you had to initiate in the first portion of Plan A was to visualize and believe.

Respond to this idea of recession that has manifested in your life with a new mind, new experience, and new voice. Now, let's get to work.

# PLAN A, PART III: BELIEF

*It is then imperative that we offer the vibration of belief and faith to support our Plan A*

***Dear God,***

*I am actually up north with one of my best friends, Brian, a week before Dia's wedding. It's a day before my formal interview with the mission agency—a day before something special will happen. I must say that being up north, connecting with nature, and simply having the moment to be still is a real privilege. You read stories from Elizabeth Gilbert and others who sojourn around the world to gain enlightenment, a newfound sense of purpose, to find themselves or other spiritual renewals. Sometimes the peace and newness we seek can easily be found in the paradise of our mind. I'm thinking back to when my journey began in New York and how drastically I have come in to my own, gained intuitive senses, and the boldness to simply be...yes, I give myself permission to be who I am. I simply am. And the more I exist without forms, labels, or projections from others, the more life opens its gates... the more heaven rains down blessings my way. I have this amazing feeling of fire or inferno in my soul. God continues to send angels of love, mercy, and strength my way...*

# CHAPTER 5:
# DO YOU HEAR THE MUSIC?

*To be embraced by life means first knowing that I embrace myself.*

One of my favorite movies of all time, *The Devil Wears Prada* serves as a constant reminder of the importance and value in truly loving yourself. In an uncanny manner, it was not the fashion dynamics that captivated my interest, but the opening credits that sparked a newfound understanding of celebration and love of self. K.T. Tunstall's song, "Suddenly I See" opens the movie, as various women appear to get ready for their workday. Yes, the fashionable frocks used to highlight numerous characters' outer beauty have their place of importance, but there was something greater permeating from the inside of the actresses being showcased that seized my attention. Juxtaposed with the following lyrics of "Suddenly I See," it almost appeared that the characters were walking to a theme song that gave them power:

*"Her face is a map of the world*
*Is a map of the world*
*You can see she's a beautiful girl*
*She's a beautiful girl*

*And everything around her is a silver pool of light*
*The people who surround her feel the benefit of it*
*It makes you calm*
*She holds you captivated in her palm...*

*I feel like walking the world*
*Like walking the world*
*You can hear she's a beautiful girl*
*She's a beautiful girl*

*She fills up every corner like she's born in black and white*
*Makes you feel warmer when you're trying to remember*
*What you heard*
*She likes to leave you hanging on her word…*

*And she's taller than most*
*And she's looking at me*
*I can see her eyes looking from a page in a magazine*
*Oh she makes me feel like I could be a tower*
*A big strong tower*
*She got the power to be*
*The power to give*
*The power to see*

*Suddenly I see (Suddenly I see)*
*This is what I wanna be*
*Suddenly I see (Suddenly I see)*
*Why the hell it means so much to me".*[3]

Do you hear the music when you wake up in the morning and begin your day? Do you hear the music permeating from your soul, outward into the world? Being one's best self and living a life that resonates with Plan A includes showing value for the person that you are. Many conversations shared with clientele that I serve begin with the question, "Do you hear the music?" After I explain what it means as they are attempting to go after their Plan A, most clients say, "No." Hearing the music is not physically waiting to hear your favorite song on your iPod or car radio. Hearing the music means that you walk your life in a steady stream of cadence that is yours alone. There is a powerful vibrational frequency of sureness, boldness, tenacity, peace, and most of all love that dwells at the

---

3   AZLyrics.com. (2000). Retrieved August 30, 2011, from http://www.azlyrics.com/lyrics/kttunstall/suddenlyisee.html

## CHAPTER 5: DO YOU HEAR THE MUSIC?

center of your humanity—and no one can either deny or grant you this special gift of 'self-love' other than you.

Loving yourself is not waiting for someone or something to give you value. Loving yourself means that you reflect your value inwardly and let it flow outwardly. How you feel about yourself has a direct effect on the expectancy of fulfilling your Plan A. The Universe acts as an energy source, directing and guiding our Plan As, but the Universe cannot fully support our individual worlds with immeasurable blessings if we do not feel deserving.

I've always known that I was very different than most men that were in my inner circle of friends and beyond, especially as an adolescent growing up in Detroit, Michigan. While most guys were into football, impressing girls, bullying peers, and the like, my focus was much different. I loved being involved in forensics (a speech competition), the arts, academics, community service, and other creative pastimes. I was a preppy guy who talked differently and was in the minority when it came to doing things in an unorthodox manner. While my brother and sister were both varsity athletes involved in various sporting activities, I was taking piano lessons, active in church youth events, and participated in minor sports undertakings.

My earliest memory as a child experiencing low self-esteem and lack of self-love is as early as kindergarten. As a result of being noticeably different at a very young age, I was teased profusely. I remember 8th graders calling me names, such as faggot, gay, punk, and sissy. This persistent form of bullying would continue until I was in high school, and it caused massive damage to my very core. Although I was vice president of my senior class, experienced leadership roles throughout my adolescent life, and was raised in a loving home, it was not enough to heal my broken soul. I used to write in a journal that I would give anything to be "normal" and see life like everyone else in my immediate surroundings. It was not until my undergrad study abroad experience in Madrid, Spain that I learned the importance of truly loving myself—all of me. I also finally understood the universal impact and consequences of not fully embracing my core.

I discovered that regardless of how "great" things appeared to be in my life, my accomplishments, and awards, there was always a steel ceiling that I would never rise above, because something was obstructing me from going beyond "good" to "great." I've always wanted authentic 'excellence' in all that I worked toward. However, the Universe cannot truly open the vault of endless possibilities unless you possess a genuine love for what has been created—you. There are no mistakes, imperfections, or inadequacies when it comes to the evolution of your being. Misunderstanding and constant denial of this truth will continuously result in the need for the lesser Plan Bs, Cs, Ds, etc., of your dreams.

While in Spain, I worked with missionaries who taught at a local seminary and led an English-speaking church. Before returning to the States, it was my job to conduct an intercultural research project on the students who migrated to Madrid. Some were facing death from apartheid, while others were simply attempting to find a means of work that could financially support their families. The constant theme that I experienced within this diverse community was: Love. Despite varied backgrounds and reasons for traveling to Spain, the community truly valued each other's existence. This community loved me for "me." They gave me temporary permission to be myself, until one day I could give myself permission to "be."

Over the course of two months, I finally took a true look in the mirror and tried to utter the words, "I love you." The first month of using this exercise was very difficult, as I did not wholeheartedly believe my words. Nonetheless, I continued every day until the repetitive expressions connected to my soul—until I could literally feel a frequency growing, emitting from my heart. Repetition in any occurrence creates muscle, whether you're physically working out or expressing a feeling. The more one exercises a muscle of thought or of the body, the more a concrete substance is created. Muscle is a force, a power, and strength. We all have an opportunity to create the experience, life, and person that we would like to become through this important muscle. Whoever says that repetition of thought, affirmations, and awareness do not create reality has unfortunately missed an opportunity to use one of the strongest mechanisms given to us.

## CHAPTER 5: DO YOU HEAR THE MUSIC?

You might be wondering, "Well, how did you finally know that you loved yourself?" Several years later I knew, because for once in my life, I did not feel the need to hide my individuality, my sexuality, my specialness, and the unique person that I am. I was proud of myself and felt an overwhelming urge to celebrate the spirit within me. The steel ceiling that had previously entrapped me began to weaken and eventually shattered. The idea of going after my Plan A was relived and I was purified as being whole.

There are various reasons why we do not love ourselves. Several potential reasons range from being molested as a child, negative views of our body images, experience of verbal and domestic abuse, to dysfunctional upbringings, and so much more. While we cannot control the mechanism that first triggered thoughts of inner loathing and destruction of love within ourselves, we do have the ability to control our response to the malady that caused it. Despite the pain, "I love me." Despite the environment, "I love me." Despite where I am in life, "I love me." Despite you, "I love me." What could really change in your life, if one day you decided that you were enough?

Now, not only do I hear the music very clearly when I rise in the morning and walk out the door, I create my own beat as well. I hear the Universe's melodic rhythm creating new and exciting passageways for me as I move closer and closer to my Plan A. I hear and feel a beat so clear that beseeches me to design my own runway in life. People might look at me and want to know the secret to my determination, self-esteem, and powerful stride. It's simple: The freedom of loving myself. Freedom in loving yourself is one expression that comes without a price tag. The freedom to love, the freedom to receive love, the freedom to share love, the freedom to be love, and the freedom to be in love are all treasures that begin with you. We will never be able to fully experience the gift of love in any form if we do not first love ourselves.

Do you hear the music?

# PLAN A, PART IV: HARD WORK

*Perseverance and hard work then carry us through the often-tumultuous journey of resistance toward fulfilling our Plan A*

*Dear God,*

*Celebration. Boldness. Expectation. Heartfelt stance. Patience. Understanding. Courage. Want. Desire. Faith. I am at a stilled place of peace, purpose, love, life, and living. God has an awesome sense of humor and an interesting manner of revealing, layer by layer, the power that lies within all of us. Awakening to my life's purpose has been an incredible task. Gosh, today reconfirmed—or rather gave me an unwavering sense—that I am in and at the right place in my life! The power of understanding and awakening to this awesome realization is remarkable. These past months have taught me about faith, our individual power, the Almighty, and love. I am at a peaceful place in my life. I understand and have strict, utmost, and relentless assurance that the desires of my heart are already met, and that awakening and accepting purpose triggers and releases the outpouring of God's love.*

# CHAPTER 6:
# THE WAITING GAME

*Patience is a virtue that will never set us up for failure.*

When we truly understand what patience is, we will not get in the way of the greatness that is yet to come. Each experience then, teaches us supportable tools, best practices and the value of being patient as we wait on our Plan A to fulfill itself. Patience is the gatekeeper for true authentic success within our Plan A. No one has been able to have long-lasting opportunities without waiting on their dreams to be fulfilled. This is another life-journey experience that serves as a shielding force to protect us while the Universe sorts out "the details" of how our Plan As should arrive. We hate it. We curse it. We deny it. We want to see ourselves arrived and relaxing in the nook of our Plan A *right now*. However, patience allows us to have the perfect moment, at the perfect time, in the perfect season, with impeccable alignment to whatever is our end goal.

Patience requires us to trust the current-day events occurring in our lives, and trust the Universe, which is at the center directing and moving events on our behalf.

One of the greatest lessons I received about the importance of patience came about through my desire to find a great apartment of my own in New York City. After I began working at a global mission agency, I moved closer to my job, into a two-bedroom condo sublet. It was a great place, had a doorman, courtyard, fitness center, and laundry on the premises, but a part of my dream or Plan A was to have my own place that was equally as nice.

One winter day, a friend of mine who lived in Brooklyn asked me if I knew of anyone looking for a roommate. He was experiencing financial problems and could no longer afford a two-bedroom apartment. I told him that I would ask around. A month later, my friend reminded me of his request and instantly, the light bulb was turned on. I could live with him! After all, I wanted to save money to find my own place and the price he suggested for rent was a steal! The only caveat was that it was very far into Brooklyn, was a difficult commute into work, and was not in a very safe community. I decided to take a chance and hope for the best, to opt for saving enough money for my own place despite obvious objections. Of course, I wanted to have my own apartment right then, but I knew that I would just have to be patient.

Fast-forward four months, and my roommate informed me that two more months before his lease was up, he was offered a studio in Chelsea for a very cheap price. The price was so amazing that he could not turn down the deal. I definitely understood! He was going to pay the second-to-last month of rent, but would either expect me to pay the entire rent for the last month, or would sublet his room for one month. I was not comfortable with the latter, so I would need to begin my search for an apartment soon, or pay the entire rent for my last month's stay. How was I going to find my Plan-A apartment in four weeks? I wasn't able to save effectively for a one-bedroom apartment in that time, especially in Manhattan. I started to freak out, but I quickly remembered how far being patient had brought me, and stopped worrying.

Two weeks later, I decided to take a glance at apartment ads online. I noticed a very unusual announcement for a one-bedroom apartment at an inexpensive price—the exact price that I wanted to pay. I looked closer at the description of the place and noticed that the photos of the view from the apartment looked exactly like my old apartment in Manhattan. After scrolling down further, there was a number listed for the apartment and a name.

## CHAPTER 6: THE WAITING GAME

"Something is strange," I thought to myself. The name listed was that of a female celebrity singer. "This is a scam!" I yelled out loud. Nonetheless, I could not turn my attention away from the photos of the apartment. I decided to call the listed number and a gentleman answered the phone. I asked about the apartment and he informed me of the address and the location. I told him that I was on my way. It was exactly 4:45 P.M. I typed the address into an internet application and a photo of the building appeared. I gasped in astonishment, excitement, and perplexity. The apartment building was across the street, directly up the block from my previous address!

After convincing a coworker and dear friend to walk over with me, I stumbled upon an amazing one-bedroom apartment with a balcony that overlooked a beautiful courtyard. The space was much bigger than I had imagined, with a doorman, caring neighbors, and for the exact price that was on my vision board. My landlord even offered me her living room furniture at no cost! At 5:00 P.M., I had sealed the deal and informed the landlord that I would take the place.

As I turned the knob and entered my new apartment, the first object that greeted me was a clay pot that said, "Hopes & Dreams." I cried. My Plan A in this regard had come true, after years of being patient with a process that I completely believed in. I immediately remembered my first year in New York, traveling from one friend's couch to another. The idea of not having a home was a very frightening undertaking when I decided to begin this journey. Despite the struggle to arrive at my end result and not knowing "how" it would come, I knew and trusted that it eventually would. If I had panicked and stepped in front of the process working out the details for me, then I would have delayed or subverted my arrival at my Plan A. Standing in my own home that first day, I understood why the journey was so important, that being faithful to the process can give us more than we could ever ask for, and that patience will always place us in the winning seat.

If we envision, develop, and release our dreams into the world, the Universe will begin to direct and move things at the speed of light. We have to remember that our time sequence is much different than God's timing. Accomplished dreams are for those who stay the course—those who persevere in the face of resistance and those who are patient enough to allow the Universe to produce the perfect outcome for our heartfelt Plan A. In this regard, my Plan A was better than what I could have possibly imagined. Every single detail that I desired in my new apartment was met and more. When we employ patience and our Plan A arrives, the last phase of arriving at the end goal will occur effortlessly. For example, as a result of my patience, I was able to find the perfect apartment in 15 minutes—the very apartment that was meant just for me. While the process may take a while, there is a special job function that the Universe is working out just for you.

Patience is timing. Timing is patience. The unforeseen things that we might not ever consider or fathom, God sees. The Universe poses questions, such as: *Are you mature enough to accept your Plan A right now? What is it that you must learn before receiving this gift? Do you believe that you are worthy of receiving your Plan A? Is there a predicament in your life that will keep you from fully embracing your dream?*

After obtaining your Plan A, look back at the course you traveled. Were you ready at the time to have your dream given to you? Were there circumstances or obstacles that haphazardly appeared? I'm certain that the answers to the above questions have caused you to rethink your position. And if so, use the example of this particular Plan A as a reference for other dreams that you cast out into the world. As a result of your experience, there should be no reason to fret or disdain the teaching methods or moments of patience. The directive that can be taken, along with other principles within this book, is *trust*. Trust that patience will always prepare you for your next goal in life.

I know firsthand that the mysteries of the world can be a frustrating experience. The waiting game can be unnerving and a trying time, forcing us to operate from a position of haste, frustration, and anger. Patience sometimes can place us at a precipice. We can either go in a direction that will give us instant gratification or travel a more difficult road and wait on the Universe to work on our behalf for Plan A to be conquered. Furthermore, it's so amazing how patient we can be with everyone else,

## CHAPTER 6: THE WAITING GAME

but not ourselves. Life is happening right now and we're so engulfed with the end result, that we've been ignoring the process. I think that it's great to back up our optimism and desires to go after our dreams with hard work and dedication, but it's also great to give our life *fun*!

Take a step back from your Plan A. Accomplishments and rewards will come while we will be oblivious to excitement for those things, if we're not enjoying the process. Go to lunch with a friend, catch a movie, meet your significant other for dinner, and release your Plan A project for the day. Remember, success is not measured on who you know, where you've been, and how quickly you obtained your dream; it's built on one's quality of life—the experiences you share and those that you care about. Patience will always serve as a teacher and a friendly guide. And today, choose to have the best quality of life possible. With patience in the background and fun checking in from the bench, let today be a wonderful day!

**Dear God,**

*"...I'm almost at a standstill, wondering which way to go in order to make these dreams come true. I don't know which direction to go. I just know that I disdain the work that I'm doing. How do I get there? I have no idea! I just need help or a directive. I feel like I've come to New York and have sacrificed a lot to be here, went through a lot in order to simply survive here, and now I'm just...waiting, waiting, and waiting once again..."*

# CHAPTER 7:
# SOMEWHERE OVER THE PERSEVERANCE RAINBOW

*It's hard not to focus on the structure or foundation of a dream that we're hoping to create. Structures give us a sense of stability and confidence. Sometimes it's more important to pay closer attention to each layer of the structure, precisely placing each brick in its intended place. Who knows? The foundation may be better than what you ever could have imagined.*

I welcomed December 1, 2010 (the last month before the swiftly approaching new year) with an eye of bewilderment and a lackluster outlook as I gazed out the 14th-floor window of my office. The day in New York City greeted us with high winds, torrential rain, and darkened clouds. If you know anything about New York City rain, you understand that no matter how full-sized your umbrella is, you're still going to get wet—it's the kind of downpour that leaves everyone drenched in water. Nonetheless, I decided to go out in the weather to have lunch and catch up with a coworker, since both of us had been out of town for most of the fall. At this time, I was still an employee at the global-based mission agency.

Returning to the building after lunch completely soaked from mid-thigh to the soles of my feet, I entered my dark office that faced an even darker exterior. Dreary days can sometimes give us a nauseating feeling of the blues, no matter where we are in our life's journey. On this day, however, an uncanny sense of joy surfaced inside me, resting on the vision and promise of my Plan A.

Oh yes, the backstory would help. I was at a crossroads in my life. The kind where the next step of unconventional purpose is received and you're ready to take the subsequent departure in life, but you're in a 'holding pattern.' It feels like you're on a fabulous plane, headed to the French Riviera, but unfortunately the pilot continuously comes on the PA system and says, "Attention passengers, we are being held by traffic control until the weather clears. Thank you for your patience." You want to take off so badly because you know that 'paradise' is in sight. However, your plane continues to sit on the runway, ever so slowly edging forward bit by bit, but never taking off. Well, that is the way I felt that day. I felt that my will to win and accomplish the end result of Plan A was vanquished or at a standstill, never to move forward again.

Just then a coworker knocked on my door and said, "You're not going to be with us much longer, are you?" I was taken aback by her question and inquired further, nonetheless answering, "No." I explained the next project that I was working on, how I've felt my Plan A in life was clear and the direction in which I would soon venture on my path. Our conversation shifted toward her life's passions and desires. I listened and then offered counsel as she asked several questions. Amazingly, the words I shared with her were what I needed to hear for my own sense of reason, reigniting the intensity of what I believed to be my Plan A. We talked about aspiring to one's life's purpose. We talked about optimism. We talked about faith. And lastly, we talked about perseverance.

I used stories from my matriculation to New York City to serve as a guide of hope for her and the new journey that she would experience, which consequently encompassed stories within my stint with homelessness. Everyone in New York appears to have what I call "the eye of the tiger." The eye of the tiger is the will and immense desire to go after one's Plan A, utilizing almost every skill possible in human endeavor. These individuals will not rest until their Plan A is accomplished, maneuvering every network, exhausting connectional resources, and not afraid

## CHAPTER 7: SOMEWHERE OVER THE PERSEVERANCE RAINBOW

of rejection. Not that other cities or places do not have that same killer instinct, but there's something rather interesting about the broad range of individuals who matriculate to the city to 'struggle' toward manifesting their Plan A. Yes, the 'Empire State of Mind' is what our modern day hip-hop society calls it.

We talked about resistance—how right at that very last millimeter you have to travel to get to your 'promised land,' there comes great turmoil and unheard of struggles in trying to move forward—that very last step that a runner has to make to cross the finish line after a marathon; or, the last note a vocalist must make, tired after months of back-to-back concerts; or, the last class a Ph.D. candidate, law school student, or grad school student, etc., has to conquer. The feeling becomes overwhelming when you have a date with destiny, but at the 11th hour, you must dig deep inside to continue. What you need is *perserverance*.

Perseverance? Yes. It's amazing how when we are seeking to accomplish our Plan A or desired dream, no one ever seems to candidly explain the importance of being able to endure the wilderness experience, known as "perseverance." At this point in the journey, your determination to succeed (perseverance) must become greater than your desire to reach your Plan A. Most of us are only interested in finding eureka in our unknown journeys, and not the will to persevere that is necessary to accomplish our Plan A. Who would have thought that pain and trepidation could really be a part of a formula to fulfill our Plan A? I surely did not. Nonetheless, resistance and discomfort in this world have seemed almost to make a bargain with our dreams—one cannot live without the other. I hear a voice loudly emitting a consistent declaration that we all sometimes appear to ignore: "No great reward comes without a bruised knee, or maybe even a bruised ego. However, proceed and enter me (perseverance) if you are bold enough to continue on this journey." Are you bold enough?

As the conversation with my coworker continued, I talked mostly about true insistence. I shared previously untold stories to encourage her, and remembered that place of passionate fire that my impatience had extinguished. Again, how could I forget the power of stillness? As our conversation came to a close, she said, "So, I needed to share my disbelief with you and have you advise me in order for you to encourage yourself, huh?" I smiled, responding, "Well…yeah!"

At the end of the day, your greatest advisor and advocate are found within. Our center is the secret place where our spirit and creator resides. Whenever we feel the need to recharge our emotional, mental, spiritual, and physical identities from the windstorms of life, there's no greater place than the source that has created us—the universal energy that abides within. Following our Plan A means understanding our never-ending source of renewed freedom whenever we need to acquire it—even if we are the culprits of our current negative circumstance.

I felt a sense of rebirth as I remembered everything that I suffered and endured during my initial time in New York City, and in beginning a lifestyle company. I also remembered in that instant that the feeling of despair was not the same as it was during my matriculation to New York. It was better, not worse. When you've experienced resistance before, it makes it easier to deal with distress when it comes again—you know what to expect, how to respond, and how to increase your faith, little by little.

Lastly, I remembered the promise "a Higher Power" gave to me when sharing my purpose and Plan A in life. I recalled how clearly I heard that voice and my response to submit and surrender. Joy resurfaced in my soul and heart. I remembered. I remembered!

Just then the storm subsided. Clouds began to move and the sun emerged again, almost as if there hadn't been a drop of rain all day. My coworker departed from my office. I turned around to my window to see a rainbow appear right before my very eyes. It was the brightest and largest rainbow I had ever seen. Various colleagues were trying to see the rainbow from their windows, but for some reason they could not. My office window was the only place where you could see this amazing kaleidoscopic vision. I could not help but remember the promise and covenant that God (in Judeo-Christian teachings) gave to Noah at the precise moment when the storm he faced subsided. The peace symbol

## CHAPTER 7: SOMEWHERE OVER THE PERSEVERANCE RAINBOW

Noah would receive—the same peace symbol I would then receive—and the end of the storm were a symbolic measure that I was offered. The most beautiful rainbow ever seen would only last for two minutes, but it was long enough for me to remember the promise given to me. After several colleagues left my office, my friend ran back in and said, "I think that was for you!"

Remember, whatever your purpose in life, whether to be a teacher, judge, engineer, mechanic, model, artist, or carpenter, only *you* can do what you were born to do. Out of all of the billions of people who exist on this planet, there is a task that only you can accomplish. How special is that? I cannot fulfill your Plan A. Your best friend, mother, brother, teacher, father, or cousin cannot perform your assignments. Only you. And it is your responsibility to respond as if your life depends on it…because it does.

**Dear God,**

*I, and so many of my dear friends, are all in major transition, every single one of us. And with transition comes complete desire to 'move forward'…now! We are all becoming impatient and waiting on the Universe to respond. God, Creator, Universe, I ask right now that for my dear friends who stand at the banks of the Red Sea, that you give us faith, patience, and calm to wait on you. Give us the courage to stand on this bank and know that your power will ultimately prevail. And I ask you to grant us miracles beyond our wildest dreams. May we remember the Red Sea and may our spirits respond with knowing, 'I can' and 'I will'…*

# CHAPTER 8:
# PLAN A FRIENDSHIPS

*Unless you're prepared to deal with "Negative Nellies," keep your dreams close (with like-minded friends) until they manifest. Try showing up and making announcements rather than asking so many negative and fearful people their thoughts about your dream!*

I know firsthand from experience that the concourse known as Plan A can sometimes be a very difficult and lonely journey. At times, I've often felt that I was supposed to venture this road alone and would need only to maintain an open relationship with God and God alone. It is often understood that the Universe is the governing agent that ultimately codirects and sustains us through every joy, moment of bewilderment, and problem that we face. However, I also believe that the Universe sends us special people in our lives to carry out an extraordinary mission and gift—the act of friendship. When I was growing up, I often heard elders say, "Choose your friends wisely. You'll be lucky if you have one good friend in life." I must respectfully disagree. Like family, I do not think we choose our friends. However, make sure that you're not confusing associates with genuine friends. Authentic friendships in our lives have a special charge and calling to perform. Have you ever experienced something in your life, later to find out that your friend is also experiencing the same thing? Regardless, if the sensation is that of joy or pain, strangely, both you and your friend(s) are collectively undertaking an experience that needed to occur in order for evolution, progression, or internal understanding to take place inside of each person. One of my best friends often tells me that I'm her sixth sense, as without fail, I call her whenever she is experiencing a difficult moment in life, and vice versa. There is usually absolutely no way I could know that something great or not so great is occurring. It's indescribable how such timely reactions with friends occur at the very second an expression is released into the world. The role of friendship within Plan A is supposed to give us a sense of renewal, acceptance, development, accountability, excitement, protection, and encouragement. Plan A friendships are sustaining mediators that act on behalf of the Universe to remind us of our humanity and connectional responsibility to fulfill our end goals, and to challenge us to boldly be our authentic selves.

After I returned to Michigan for the second time, I quickly started working to develop a business plan, website content, etc., and worked tirelessly for months to make my way to New York, as I felt it was the place for me. I remember talking to a good friend of mine that I trusted to share my Plan A with—telling her that I just need to get so much in order before I leave, have enough money, find this or that, and she responded, "But Klay, that's just it. It will never be enough for all of the variables to be met. How many people do we know that said, 'Once this is in order, I'll go,' and it is now 10 years later? You just have to go!" That was the best advice I could have received. It was the last factor that I would need to catapult my Plan A to another level. Plan A friendships support our dreams and goals without fearful questions of discouragement and unconstructive views of advancement.

I have learned that there is something very unique about Plan A friendships that a lot of people may not understand—sacrifice. Friendships through this form of purposeful understanding are willing to sacrifice in order for one to arrive at his or her calling. When I arrived in New York and traveled between housing, I experienced sustaining love from Plan A friends that I will never forget. One afternoon in the winter of 2008, I ventured with my friend to a grocery store, to take a break from networking. As we were strolling down several aisles, I noticed that she placed two of everything in her basket. Finally, I asked her if she was stocking up for the winter and she replied, "No, these are for you." I was very grateful for the wonderful gesture that she offered. Shortly after leaving the grocery store, she received a phone call from another friend confirming plans for the evening. Surprisingly, my friend cancelled her outing. I wondered to myself, "Did she cancel her plans as a result of spending her extra cash on me?" I felt compelled to ask her and she replied, "Yes, and I do not want to hear anything from you. This journey that is your own is just as important to me as it is for you. We're done here." And this response would begin to trickle down from every member of my Plan A friendships.

In another instance of friendship, a great friend who was a graduate student in North Carolina understood the level of stress and anxiety that I was suffering at the time and sent for me. I took a full week break in her lovely home and became reacquainted with nature. We made meals together, reminisced about old times, worked out, rented movies, stayed up late, and talked for hours. During that trip I slept more peacefully than I had in months. Of course, my inquisitive mind asked her, "Why did you feel compelled to send for me?" She said, "Because I wanted you to get a good night's sleep." When you're experiencing Plan A friendships, there is a common shared bond that is unbreakable, regardless of geographical location. The Universe will bind Plan A friendships to us and give more support than we could ever fathom, as long as we boldly respond to the call of our Plan A.

As you begin your Plan A journey, consider the following in regard to your friendships:

1. Authentic friendships do not require explanation as to why you want a better life; they just support it.

2. Assess the energy of others before you share your dreams. You do not want everyone's energy clouding your end result or Plan A.

3. Sometimes it's better to just show up and make announcements instead of consulting with others—this is also true with family members.

4. Unfortunately, not everyone is happy for individuals who not only *want* better for their lives, but actually *walk* into their destiny.

5. Sometimes the journey along the path of accomplishing our dreams can be a very lonesome expedition, but Plan A friendships will always be there for support when you need it.

6. Plan A friendships celebrate the accomplishments of others—because when *you* win, *I* win; we *all* win. Your blessing is also mine.

7. Real community comes from those who support your ambitions and dreams. If you find yourself in constant opposition and explanation with those who claim to have your best interests at heart, then maybe it's time to reevaluate your community.

8. Believe people when they demonstrate their support or non-support of you. Plan A friendships are not relationships that are forced.

9. Jealousy is a real plague in our world. Nevertheless, it's not up to us to speak venom on someone's name, even if they are in the wrong. Pray, meditate, and send out positive energy for those who are attempting to understand something or someone that is different—namely your new realization of going after your Plan A.

10. Understand that not everyone has the courage to say to another, "That's a great opportunity that you were given. I'm curious, how did you get there? Can you teach me? Do you mind if I ask you questions about your Plan A, direction or vision that you've accepted for your life?"

Remember that Plan A friendships are based on a spiritual connection. We must trust our energy and the direction that the Universe will inevitably show us in regard to discovering our Plan A friendships. Relationships within this understanding offer support through various methods of giving, and are not merely restricted to the manner of my own experience. Support is support, however it manifests itself in our lives through sustaining Plan A friendships. There is absolutely no way that I could list the countless blessings of love and support that I have received from my Plan A friends. However, I know without a doubt that I would not be where I am today without their hands of watchfulness, hearts of grace, minds of patience, and giving souls. It is important that we offer gratitude for the placement of such remarkable people in our lives and remember to return the favor, when it's our turn to be a Plan A friend to another.

***Dear God,***

*__I have a secret.__*

*Shhh…conceal it inside.*
*Shhh…inhalation from within….*
*Shhh…don't release the wind…the wind of destruction, separation, and pain…the dressing that covers the bruise of disclosure…the asylum that protects it…your secret.*

*You've moved violently through your limited days, resisting the beast that dwells in your soul…the monstrous fiend of biblical times that hounds the streets of Corinth.*

*Rock hard feeling…sentiment and sensation pursues the visual physique of the mortal that provides nourishment to your palate of fascination.*

*Heartbreaking discretion and dutiful murmurs of rejection irk the creature that usher screams inside your body of containment.*

*Never-ending bliss, lifelong nurturing, sexual aggression, and soundless pain bequeath your heart of embarrassment.*

*Whispers. Stares. Judgment. Confusion and hate remain in the swagger of your damaged stride. But you gently whisper....*

*Shhh...conceal it inside.*
*Shhh...inhalation from within....*
*Shhh...don't release the wind...the wind of destruction, separation, and pain...the dressing that covers the bruise of disclosure...the asylum that protects it...your secret.*

*Mind warp. Twilight Zone. Panic. Protection is found only in the respite of solitude and spiritual regulation from the universe of hallucination. Tender prayers and heartfelt tears of freedom hide the beauty of your shadowed silhouette.*

*The end. Help. Smother. Your restless nights add maturity to your adolescent body of past perfection and crumpled linen to your hills of collapsed smiles.*

*Beg. Kaput. Future. The walls of Jericho have finally tumbled down. Armageddon has inaudibly pierced the small crevice between your lips.*

*Furtive. Hush-hush. Covert. It's finally out. Ancient times are no more. Contemporary art hangs from the gray wall. Picturesque visions of Black and White surface. Immortal quietness no longer dwells within your clandestine spirit.*

*Numbness. Fear. Hope.*

*Shhh…conceal it inside.*
*Shhh…inhalation from within….*
*Shhh…don't release the wind…the wind of destruction, separation, and pain…the dressing that covers the bruise of disclosure…the asylum that protects it…your secret.*

# CHAPTER 9:
# PARDON ME

*Give to others forgiveness and in turn, the Universe will give you back your life.*

Forgiveness is the greatest spiritual experience in which humans could ever participate. When we forgive we produce a channel or pathway, if you will, into the Universe that not only heals our broken souls but also adds a measure of healing into the world. If we all practiced measures of forgiveness, it could inevitably rid the world of wars, disease, violence, and all forms of evil as we know it. Any form of disruption to us uplifting and offering joy in our world is the result of some kind of fracture. Just as in the corporal body, all fractures, wounds, or incisions must be healed in order to return to their original state—in order to regain full functionality and "life." So, what happens when our emotional fractures do not heal as a result of our unwillingness to forgive? Forgiveness is a connectional system that offers love. Love then offers healing, wholeness, restoration, and completion back into the damaged system of life. And finally, the current of forgiveness returns to the individual who first casted out the request, ultimately purifying and restoring fullness to his or her life. Failure to respond in the spirit of forgiveness can result in an empty life of attempting to reach the vision of Plan A, but ultimately never fulfilling the dream. What would change if I told you that exercising the act of forgiveness propels you closer to your Plan A?

Many of us might not believe this idea that forgiveness plays a significant role in the process of fulfilling our Plan A. No problem, we are all entitled to our opinions. However, what does the body have to say about forgiveness? A further demonstration of the effects of not forgiving can be found in the reaction of the human body. The physical body is the place that captures our emotions and can potentially serve as a snapshot of where we are mentally, emotionally, and spiritually in our lives. When there is a rift in a relationship—whether platonic, romantic, or self-inflicted—the need for forgiveness oftentimes will manifest in our physical bodies as unhealthy toxic disorders. Examples include random acne outbreaks, excessive weight gain, or bodily ailments, which all serve as indicators that something internally is troubled or in pain. Forgiveness usually plays a major part within this sequence of pain. When we are resentful toward another, hold grudges, and are unable to grant forgiveness, our physical bodies (our shell) have no place to release the tension. Our pain then becomes lodged in our bodies, and manifests in some form of poisonous residue. Of course, we might seek out weekly visits to our local spa or chiropractor to cope with the physical pain rather than examine the underlying emotional pain. But this path leads to our pockets continuously being emptied and our lives dragging stagnantly forward with the misinformed idea that "My miracle and Plan A is on its way."

This is one of the greatest red flags present to inform us that something is not quite right within, but we unfortunately ignore this particular sign and go on with our everyday schedule, wondering why we are unable to progress and move beyond our current state. I never quite understood the effects of forgiveness until I experienced the most horrifying occurrence of my life, while a graduate student at Princeton Seminary. I had no idea that what would soon transpire would set a precedent for how I approach situations as relates to forgiveness.

The hallowed halls of Princeton Seminary welcomed students from all over the world with varied interests, perspectives, and reasoning for pursuing theological studies. I met many students and heard their fascinating life journeys, but one student would inevitably change my life forever. Kyle was an interesting guy, witty, intelligent, and charismatic. He had a very intriguing presence that was jovial, yet demanded respect.

## CHAPTER 9: PARDON ME

He and I would see each other from time to time as we shared several survey courses, but did not ultimately become friends until a month or so after classes began. Once we realized that we had a lot in common, we started to study together, hang out, and open up about various life experiences that were difficult. We were becoming closer and closer as the year progressed. Unexpectedly, we fell in love with one other. It was the first same-sex interaction for both of us, which naturally frightened us, as we were each taught that gay relationships were wrong and ungodly. At several points within our interaction, we abruptly stopped communicating with one another, but discovered that our love would outweigh any notion of disgust or shame that we felt throughout our association.

After our first-semester finals, we decided to take a road trip to visit Kyle's family in the state of Tennessee. During our trip, we spent a lot of time with Kyle's father, a Pentecostal pastor. Throughout our stay, we disguised our association as being close friends, but his father would soon find out that we were more than friends. After returning to New Jersey, I received a phone call from Kyle's dad ridiculing, accosting, and chastising me for "forcing his son into gay activity." As the conversation reached its hateful peak, I heard the words, "Don't you know that I can banish your soul to hell?" I felt an immediate jolt of pain, anger, and immobility that I had never experienced before. It was as if time stood still and my soul did not exist any longer. At the time I was so ashamed of myself for "allowing" such a "crime" to happen.

Kyle's father would continue to harass and try to control me through insulting phone calls, and used the name of God to serve as the catalyst for what would be my damnation if I did not change. I had no idea what to do, since all of this was new to me and I kept it to myself for quite some time. I stopped eating, lost weight, failed a class (threatening academic probation), and started to lose my hair. Kyle's father forbade him to communicate with me and his wish was granted. I was barely 22 years old and Kyle's father definitely used my adolescence to his advantage. Later that year, my relationship with Kyle dissolved, and the harassment stopped.

For the next two years, Kyle's father's words would haunt me in my day-to-day interactions and even when I closed my eyes to recharge at night. Once I started to rediscover my self-worth, I regained a sense of consciousness and inner strength that allowed me to revisit this situation and understand clearly what had occurred. The pain that I experienced converted into rage and anger. I had disdain for Kyle's dad and wanted him to suffer the same pain that he caused me. But, what I did not understand at the time was that my contempt for him and inability to forgive caused me more strife in other personal relationships, life opportunities, and future advancement in general. The anger-fueled energy I directed at him appeared to redirect itself towards me. How could I expect positive prospects of any kind to enter my world when I was repeatedly sending out messages of hate?

None of this occurred to me until one day I received an email news blast from Kyle's father, showcasing a website for his new church. I then realized how quickly he had moved on with his life. Kyle's father was not in the least bit immobilized, while I was holding onto resentment and other ill feelings. I was functioning as if this painful experience had happened yesterday. I finally understood that my mind, soul, and heart were holding onto what was just a memory of what had happened. My ill feelings were continuously released toward a person who was no longer in confrontation with me. Life had moved on for Kyle's father. Therefore, my feelings of hatred functioned as a boomerang, returning back to me. When I experienced this epiphany, I took a moment to remember the grievance, allowed myself to feel the pain, and released a statement of forgiveness into the world. And then I forgave myself for harboring such feelings and asked the Universe to clear my heart of any feelings of disgust.

The more I became conscious of the need to forgive others, the better I started to feel about my quality of life, my future, and Plan A in general. There is a strange feeling of peace that is hard to explain when we release negative feelings that others have caused us. I felt closer to my true self, friends, family, and God. I am also very sure that when we do forgive, it brings us closer to fulfilling our Plan A. Life in general is easier and people cordially extend their hands of grace toward us when we are the offenders. I have experienced some of the most remarkable, intelligent,

## CHAPTER 9: PARDON ME

creative, and talented people whose abilities alone place them in another league. Nonetheless, as a result of their failure to forgive others, their Plan As will never be actualized, but will instead remain simple thoughts that were once novel ideas.

Gain back your power, reestablish your inner peace, and grant yourself the opportunity to further expand the cycle of life to all those who come in contact with you. Not only will you increase the likelihood of fulfilling your Plan A, but you will also give the world a boost of regenerated love and support that will return to you when you least expect it.

**Dear God,**

*I love myself. I am beautiful, a wonderful guy, and a treasure! I am a magnificent businessman, writer, speaker, friend, son, uncle, giver, supporter, confidant, brother, best friend, advocate, and so many other great things that reside close to my heart. All is well and I believe it and in me!*

# CHAPTER 10:
# DOWN WITH THE KING

*Dreams fulfilled require us to operate from a place of complete, unrelenting, and unapologetic AUTHORITY.*

For a great percentage of my early life, I accepted a burden that most people have or will experience in their lifetime: "How does the world see me?" I used to view several life occurrences with questions such as: "Will 'they' accept me? Am I good enough? How will my gifts and talents support the group that I am trying to fit into?" Rather than asking myself, "How does a particular person, place, or experience support my Plan A?" I consistently focused on acceptance as an external force that someone would need to give me.

When we are attempting to live out our Plan As, one of the most difficult notions to avoid is promoting kingship with the various crowds that we come in contact with. By placing others in a state of kingship, we are not only relinquishing our abilities to be present but we are unknowingly transmitting a signal to the universe that says, "I do not believe I am deserving of this dream or desire I am attempting to fulfill." We are placing such emphasis on trying to fit other peoples' mode or model of our Plan A that we place people on pedestals—giving them more power than our Plan A or the Universe that gave us our dream. No wonder then, that one day you may wake up and find that you've moved west, when your intention was to head east. Moving in a manner of authority allows us to create the Plan A experiences that we are attempting to reach. The path full of resistance is more bearable when we understand our own power and authority in whatever path we are attempting to navigate.

For most of my professional experiences, I seemed to have always functioned within a management role. I was usually the youngest executive on my team, supervising individuals old enough to be my parents' age, or sometimes my grandparents' age. I made it a standard practice never to tell my staff or colleagues how old I was, with the mindset that my age would prevent individuals from respecting me as a managerial executive. While earning respect as a result of youthful age has its place in some professional settings, I used this false premonition as a means to mask my insecurity. Sometimes, it is much easier to mislead ourselves, especially if we are convinced of a certain disillusion and believe it at our very core. It is also more dangerous for us to be the bearer of our own lies. Because we are the sole individuals who created the falsehood, it also means that the root of our deception is lodged far deeper than what another individual could plant. Our mistruths of where we are in life can be damaging and perpetuate a self-inflicted cycle of stagnation— ultimately forming a blockage to our Plan A.

Some time ago, I was approached to be on a panel for an international nonprofit organization that was hosting a career development conference for low-income women reentering the workforce. I was excited for the opportunity to be a part of the conference and panel. The panel, entitled, "How to Find Your Purpose In Life," would feature individuals who have expertise in this area; a question and answer portion was also entailed. One week before the scheduled event, I received a finalized agenda showcasing top professionals from around the world who would lead various talks and discussions. I scrolled down to my assigned panel discussion and noticed that next to the theme was a sole individual's name to present—my name. I thought, "This must be a mistake." Ten minutes later I received an email informing me that my session had changed to a plated-lunch talk and that I would be the keynote speaker. "Wait!" I said to myself. "I am not prepared to be the only speaker!" Was that really a point of concern for me? Or was it more that I was petrified

## CHAPTER 10: DOWN WITH THE KING

to speak in front of world executive leaders, who were kings to me, and fail in front of them? Yes, that sounds more like it.

Going into the session, I was extremely nervous and trembling inside. The night before I was only able to sleep for about three hours, as my uneasy mind traveled to the same question within kingship: "How does the world see me?" Ironically, I prepared a talk to introduce my philosophy of Plan A to the world. The conference would be the first time that I would publicly address this area of work in a communal forum.

When I entered the ballroom, my two gracious hosts for the day welcomed me and treated me like a king. In fact, it seemed that everyone that I came in contact with was treating me as if I was very special, regal, and a leader. Could it be that I am very special? Regal? A leader? As I took my seat, I laughed to myself as thoughts of, "This is what I was born to do" surfaced in my mind. I decided there and then that I would die to the kings that I had manifested in my life, and from now on would value the purpose and calling that I've been tasked with. After all, this is what Plan A is all about, right? "Enough!" I said to myself. "I am here to help change lives and speak to the very best of my ability." And I did just that. I released the theme of kingship and spoke about Plan A as only I could. By the end of my talk, the audience was in tears and offered gratitude for motivating, empowering, and encouraging radical revolution in their lives. Little did the group know that sharing this extraordinary moment with them had in turn caused me to begin to extinguish this idea of kingship that I had bred and nurtured for years.

Later, I remember having a conversation with my mentor that served as the last action of assault that I would need to forever vanquish the "King." He said, "I'm going to say something here. Please indulge me. It seems that we are constantly revisiting this idea of wondering how others will accept and/or receive you. If I place my hand in the air, as if it's a magic wand, it is simply giving you permission to not worry anymore about how you're being received. This is what you want, correct?" I answered, "Yes." (I was puzzled at his question and response, but wanted to understand where he was going). He then waved his hand and responded, "Then just be...it. Just be." Wow. Just be? Yes. Just *be*.

Ironically, the answer was simple. I wanted to change something that was preventing me from reaching my Plan A. I think that occasionally we search for so many methods to cleanse, protect, and change us when the answer to altering our current circumstance is a humble internal mindset of: "Just be." Whatever is in your life performing the role of "King," know that you have the power to demolish the pedestal and regain your authority. The same mindset that created external "royal courts" has the same propensity to destroy them.

*Dear God,*

*I have not written in some time. So much has happened and a lot of new goals have been established. My last day at the agency is next Friday, April 29th. It's crazy because I feel like a revolution is happening inside of me. I guess it feels like my dreams, with all of my hard work, have come true. I've been experiencing a lot of fullness lately, in the sense of feeling overwhelmed, but in a good way. It's kind of like when you've been waiting for something to happen for so long that when it does you can't say anything verbally, but your heart is screaming, "Thank you, God!" I know my words may be insufficient at the present moment, but I'm so overwhelmed that I can't say anything else. My vision board is moving because I am moving in a good way, recognizing my value for real. I think that because I do recognize my value, it's not surprising to me how great God works—that thing, that power, entity, being that lives inside of me is meeting me at my center. The ultimate way for us to experience the Sacred is by being vulnerable with and to ourselves. There, God resides and our center is healed. It's restored. It's set on fire, and what we can do is endless. And this I've experienced and know for sure…*

# CHAPTER 11:
# IT'S NEVER TOO MUCH

*The dream of there and then is lodged in the here and now. Be your best physical self today.*

While working hard to nourish our internal self is important, it is also essential that we recognize the significance in being physically ready for our Plan A. Envisioned opportunities and desired dreams arise without notice, requiring us to be gracious hosts, always prepared, and ready for unexpected company, namely, 'success.' Have you ever received a serendipitous phone call for a job opportunity, audition, blind date, or participation in a contest and declined the offer because you were simply not physically ready? Maybe it's the pesky 25 pounds that you'd like to lose, or the shaggy hair that is in desperate need of a cut, or the discolored white dress shirts that you need to replace. Whatever your story might be, living out Plan A means that we also invest in our physical appearance through effective exercise, eating nutritional foods, and maintaining a neat appearance. Plan A does not require us to be in the most expensive designer labels, be a member of an elite gym, or have a weekly standing appointment at a luxury spa. However, Plan A does suggest that we take care of our external body to the very best of our ability and within our financial means. Plan A demands that we reflect our substance through our style. The idea is not to be perfect, but if we want to attract a completely better life, then we must do the work necessary in all realms to accomplish our dreams.

One of my favorite conversations of all time took place on a New York City subway during rush hour. It's virtually impossible to not overhear conversations at the peak of New York's highest travel time. A woman who appeared to be in her mid-thirties was chatting with her girlfriend about the kind of guy that she wanted to attract. Her list ranged from a great physical body, awesome personality, prideful in his appearance, to a level of spirituality that peaked her interest. After about five minutes of conversation, her friend stopped her and said, "Well, that sounds really great, but what will he think of you when he meets you?" She replied, "Well, he'll think I'm awesome, of course!" Nodding in agreement, her girlfriend continued, "Of course he will; you have an amazing personality and spirit! But, you're interested in this physically fit, well-groomed guy who takes pride in his appearance and such. Well, this might sound harsh, but you really do not take the time necessary to put your best foot forward in a physical sense. Do you know what I mean? If like attracts like, then he may not be interested in you."

Initially, I thought her girlfriend was rude and unpleasant with her comments. Then it occurred to me that she was correct in highlighting the overall importance of being physically ready to receive an ideal candidate for a romantic relationship in this regard. Based on her desires for the relationship she sought, she also would need to be what she preferred to attract. This idea extends to job opportunities, artistic aspirations, and to whatever area your dream of Plan A will take you. It's imperative to be physically ready right now for the end goal. We might have gasped at the brutal delivery of her friend's honest assessment, but in the grand scheme of things, she proved to be a real friend. In this case, we find a woman interested in attracting a certain kind of person in her life when she didn't take care of her own physical self. As the conversation progressed, the woman admitted that she did not put forth her best effort, attributing this state to laziness. However, the effort that we give toward our Plan A is the effort and result that will be given back to us.

Next, it is important to be conscious that dressing the part serves as a form of progression. After styling clients, sometimes they will ask me, "Are you sure this isn't too much?" I usually reply with, "It's never too much!" I realized that when most people ask this question, it's never

## CHAPTER 11: IT'S NEVER TOO MUCH

about them truly believing that the clothing is inappropriate for the function of engagement, that it does not fit their physique well, or is not their particular kind of style; it's more that the individual lacks the confidence to boldly be the person that he or she has asked to become.

One particular client was making a transition from graduate school to Wall Street and inquired about my services. He spoke about his Plan A of becoming an investment banker and asked for my company's help in styling him. At his first fitting, he initially frowned upon the attire that I selected. He said, "Well, the suits look really nice, but this is not what a coordinator wears." I replied, "Precisely. You do not want to look like a coordinator; you want to be an investment banker. That's your Plan A!" Operating from a place of being in the proposed role right now projects us onto the shore of our Plan A. Not only does looking our best help us get noticed, it also increases our self-confidence, which in turn strengthens us in other capacities of our professional existence. The domino effect is contagious and could potentially inspire others to present their best to the world as well.

Being our best physical self also means that we get plenty of exercise and eat healthy foods. We are conscious about the things that we put in our body and work hard to preserve it's healthy nature. Please do not confuse Plan A with suggesting that everyone needs to be a perfect model sample size or become a vegetarian for the rest of their lives. However, being physically fit and healthy protects the longevity of our Plan A, as our outer shell is the mechanism that will carry us along each place and moment we will experience. If we're not physically healthy, within our means of preparation, we will not be able to properly respond when opportunities, challenges, and resistance arise.

During the second month after my arrival in New York, I started to develop a traditional winter sniffle that turned into a severe cold. At the time I was staying at one of my "in-between" homes in New Jersey and living without insurance. My innocent sniffle turned into a painful cough, which turned into an upper-respiratory problem, which then turned into an explosive flu. There appeared to be a steady decline and without any option left, I drove myself to the hospital in Princeton. I'm not sure what I was thinking at the time of venturing to a medical center without insurance, but I believed that the hospital would have mercy on me, since I had been a student in that area the year prior. I was wrong. They definitely sent me an invoice for services rendered.

Nonetheless, the doctor at the hospital did confirm that I was neither nourishing my body properly nor receiving sufficient hours of sleep. She expressed that until I maintained consistent care of my physical form, I would remain sick. Another Plan A friend reached out to me and offered me a room at a hotel that she managed for as long as I needed to recover. She brought me food from special events that she coordinated at the hotel, plenty of liquids to hydrate my sick body, and constant prayers for a speedy recovery. I do not remember being that sick before while living on the east coast. I remember telling God that I would do anything if the Spirit would send provisions to heal me.

After a week or so at the hotel with constant care, I was able to recover and get back to the mission of going after my Plan A. Ironically, my body first responded in a subtle message sent through sniffles. As if having the sniffles was not enough for me to understand what was occurring, my body continued to send more severe messages to get my attention, and it finally did, bringing all activity to a halt. I also did not effectively exercise at all and was granted an opportunity for a free gym membership at the local YMCA. I did not take the gift of having a healthy body seriously and completely ignored being my best in this regard.

Plan A tells us to listen to our bodies and feel the energy that it's seeking to give us. Our bodies are the central communication hub that transmits and receives signals from our mental, emotional, and spiritual properties. These properties will always check in with us, letting us know where we are in life, and possibly asking us to take a break, nourish, exercise, clean, and repair.

There are multidimensional understandings and deductions as to why preparing our physical frames for success is imperative for displaying Plan A readiness. Our best physical appearance tells the world that we take our quality of life seriously and are ready to receive the blessings that

## CHAPTER 11: IT'S NEVER TOO MUCH

we desire. Beyond presenting an immaculate exterior for our intended Plan A, the entity beneath our clothing must be cherished, appreciated, and carefully supported. It's never too much to consistently show up as your very best physical self. Do not concern yourself with wondering how others will receive you. You're on a Plan A mission and understand the importance of maintaining excellence in your physical life! As a result of investing in your physical Plan A, your level of endurance will be heightened, igniting an exhibition of vigor in other areas of your life. Your discipline and diligence in being your best physical self will pay off and offer you power to cross the finish line in style.

**Dear God,**

*What was the best part of my day? Hearing my friend take back his life and joy manifest in his heart; helping him get there. I am thankful for peace, friendship, love, and strength of mind and character; for my parents and sister and brother; for life; and also for the abundance of gifts the Universe has and will share with me.*

# CHAPTER 12:
# THANK YOU. MORE PLEASE.

*Let the light of another day be enough.*

Mastering the art of gratitude is very difficult when we're faced with countless levels of adversity in almost every direction we turn. Like various other principles of Plan A, gratitude is often a missing link when it comes to understanding its importance in propelling us closer to our Plan A. Gratitude does not only act as a driving vehicle, it also serves as a mechanism that absorbs the aftershocks of experiencing resistance. In conversations I've shared, I've learned that most of the clients I work with don't understand why not developing gratitude for where we are in life at the moment has anything to do with our desired path and moving forward toward our Plan A.

Before my New York experience, I really did not understand the value of gratitude and how beneficial practicing this form of spirituality can be. After one of my housing changeovers, from a friend's home in New Jersey to another friend's home in New York, I stumbled upon the meaning of gratitude in an unusual way. I noticed that my car's gas level was approaching E. I had $30.00 in my pocket to last me for maybe a couple of days. I paid for $10.00 in gas, remembered that I would need to pay two tolls, and then realized that I had not eaten breakfast or lunch.

I was headed to Pizza Hut Bistro when I saw the golden arches of

McDonald's just next door. I turned into the parking lot of McDonald's and proceeded to the drive-thru window, yet recalled a promise that the Universe made to me before I set off on my journey. Within my frenzy of worries, shortly before I left Michigan to return east, my main concerns were shelter and food. How would I eat and would I have healthy food? Where would I live? These were questions that plagued my mind before my expedition. My anxiety was settled by a promise that I did not hear or see, but felt. As soon as I commenced to worry about housing and nourishment before leaving Michigan, I felt a reassurance at my core—almost as if a promise was made clear to me from God, with a signature written on my heart, reassuring me that I would never go without shelter or nutritious food.

While poised at the drive-thru window at McDonald's, I remembered that promise and decided to drive next door to Pizza Hut Bistro. I was ready to order a "heart healthy" vegetable pizza, when a worker informed me that the drive-thru window was for corporate orders only and directed me toward an entryway. I said, "Thank you," and drove back across the street to McDonald's. Clearly, this was a sign that I could not afford Pizza Hut Bistro, but could manage at McDonald's. I approached the ordering station at the drive-thru of McDonald's and surveyed their menu. But I rapidly grew impatient and angry, because I felt that the Universe was starting to let me down. McDonald's was not a part of the promise! Beyond my feelings of anger, I became ungrateful and started to complain. I switched gears to drive and set off, yet again, to Pizza Hut Bistro. After parking my car and walking inside, a bubbly waitress greeted me and said, "Oh, next time you can use the door to your left. It's closer." I said, "Okay," and then placed an order for a veggie pizza and was seated in the waiting area.

I then received a phone call from a business associate who was also complaining about her job and apartment. I thought to myself, "What are you complaining about? At least you have a place of your own and a steady-paying job." After I consoled her via phone, I felt humbled and a sense of shame. Here I was advising her on something that I was not doing well. I quietly concluded my call with her as a waitress motioned me over to the counter to collect my veggie pizza. Once I reached the counter, the

## CHAPTER 12: THANK YOU. MORE PLEASE.

perky waitress said, "Here's your pizza. Thank you, have a great day," and pushed the pizza toward me. I said, "Thank you," as I retrieved my wallet from my pants pocket. She said again, "Thank you, have a great day," and edged the pizza closer to me. I hastily said, "No, thank you. What is the total?" Then she leaned across the counter, gently placing the pizza in my hand, and said in a more direct voice, "No sir. Thank you. Here is your vegetable pizza." In shock, I replied, "Thank…you." She maintained her controlled voice and said, "Next time, just remember to enter through the same door that you exit." I walked toward the door, turned around to say thank you again, and she was gone. Eventually, I returned to my car and ate my pizza while silently weeping.

My mind started to race in an attempt to understand what had just happened. How did she know that I really could not afford a pizza? It couldn't be my appearance, I thought to myself. I was nicely dressed, in a suit and tie. Did she overhear the conversation I had with my business associate? But I was very quiet and spent my time encouraging her, I reasoned. How did she know? And what did she mean when she said, "Next time, just remember to enter through the same door that you exit"? While I tried to figure out what the logical explanation for this occurrence could be, a peaceful calm met my anxious mind. I thought, "Why does it matter how you came to receive such a great gift? Is it really important if she thought you were poor, overheard your conversation, or any other questioning?" The lesson behind this opportunity was yes, that of faith, but more importantly, gratitude. It was important not to question the "how's," but to respond with "Thank you."

Later, I interpreted the comments of the waitress as a reminder to be just as grateful before, during, and at the end of my journey, regardless of what occurred. The same mechanism that granted me access to a world of dreams would be the same sustaining factor to get me through. Gratitude is a spiritual exercise that allows us to vanquish resistance at its highest level of assault. It has the ability to numb and annihilate outside worldly forces that tempt us to give up on our Plan A. Consequently, Plan A asks us the ultimate question of faith: Can we be just as joyous and content when we're at the top of our rainbows and also when we're experiencing ghastly lows in life? I forgot the importance of giving gratitude to God for the things that I did have. I had a reliable and warm car, decent clothing, caring friends, and good health, among other things. The practice of writing words of gratitude in my journal before I went to bed at night and started my day was rendered null and void. I had departed from the exercise and discipline of offering thanks for the good that was occurring.

Plan A says, "I may not be where I want to go right now, but in the interim I will be grateful for the present moment." The present moment is all that we have and if we look closely at our individual lives, there is probably a multitude of things that are right as compared to things that are wrong. In relation to the world of gratitude, a client once said, "You're absolutely right. I should be thankful for the present moment and the good in my life. There is always someone with a worse situation." I agree, but why must it take looking at another's unfortunate circumstance for us to know that we are blessed beyond measure with what we do have?

# PLAN A, PART V: SURRENDER

*After doing everything humanly possible to accomplish our goal, we must surrender our dream and trust in a higher power to realize our Plan A*

**Dear God,**

*I am feeling a sense that things are coming together; like the storm is subsiding and the waves are effortlessly trying to simply do what they do…flow. I'm assuming that maybe this is what life looks like when one allows the process to take place—life just flows. I am really trying to flow these days, because with so much out of my control, the least that I can do is trust the one thing that I know to be true…letting go in order to let life flow.*

*…I sit here and look at every nook and cranny of my vision board and see so much potential and certain destiny. I've always felt that I have been able to envision my success before it happens; I believe in that force, and I know that my creative passion is in real alignment with who I am. I do believe that for me, a lot—or most actually—of the life that I want or choose to have is all intertwined: love, finances, home, calling. I am present here and I'm ready to really let go and open up to the Universe in order for my real dreams to come true…*

# CHAPTER 13:
# I SURRENDER ALL

*After you've done all that you can, don't just 'stand,' but SURRENDER and allow the process to construct the 'how' for you.*

Defeated? Exhausted? Had enough? On the brink of giving up? Good idea. Give "it" up to something higher than yourself to bring about your Plan A. This is a major part of your growth within the journey to arrive at your Plan A. Whenever I mention the process of surrendering to clients that I work with, most of them confuse the idea of releasing their 'dream' with:

1. Giving up on their Plan A.

2. Suggesting that hard work is not important within the process.

3. Believing that they are not good enough to achieve their Plan A.

4. Believing that surrendering is a form of weakness.

5. Fearing that surrendering means that they are not a part of the process.

6. Believing that surrendering is a form of laziness.

7. Thinking some kind of unknown magical force will carry out their task.

8. Believing that they cannot trust anyone more than themselves.

9. Thinking that surrendering is only for religious people.

10. Fearing that no one will hear their plea for help.

While the above fears associated with surrendering barely graze the surface of internal concerns and conflicts that we might have with releasing our Plan A to something higher than ourselves, there comes a point where our physical, mental, emotional, and spiritual beings can no longer carry the torch to our end goal. I am reminded of the ceremonious event that transpires before each Olympic Games. A diplomat of the hosting city is selected to run, transporting a flamed torch to the next stationed person, who in turn runs to transfer the flame to the next stationed person, and so on until finally the last runner has lit the Olympic Cauldron. This is an example of what surrendering looks like. Passing on the flame and releasing governance to the next person is trusting that they will carry out the function until the goal is achieved. The runners' willingness to allow another vessel—most often unknown to them—to carry a precious gift is the same custom that the Universe is waiting to do for you.

After you have done all that you can possibly do in the name of your Plan A—worked exceptionally hard, hustled, wept, and any other method within your scope of human knowledge—relieve yourself of your burden and allow the "Knowledge of all Knowledge" to work on your behalf. Surrendering is not only the most difficult task to accomplish within your journey to achieving your Plan A, it is also typically the last phase within the voyage that most people will experience, potentially stretching over a long period of time. Life would be vastly easier if we allowed ourselves to give all areas of anxiety that occur to the Universe within the first moment we set out to accomplish something. Nonetheless, we continue to be our very own gladiator, when there's a knight in shining armor ready to step in and toil on our behalf. Understanding the process of surrendering was not very clear to me until the experience of New York City.

As stated before, I was practically living out of my car, finding odd-end

## CHAPTER 13: I SURRENDER ALL

jobs and opportunities to make money—literally floating between friends' homes for close to a year. Toward the end of that time, I did secure housing on my friend's couch. I moved my clothes from another friend's home to create a makeshift closet in the attic of my new temporary home. I could tell that the weight of the clothes might be too much for the portable closet, but didn't pay it too much attention.

As money issues would arise, my energy level became lower and lower. I was emotionally broken, felt a sense of defeat, and wondered how much more I could take. I started to freelance for a retail company as a visual stylist—often working as late as 3 a.m. Unfortunately, New York City has a reputation for paying freelance artists in a less-than timely fashion. It literally took two months for me to receive a check for my services. By that point, I was virtually living off of $25.00 a week.

One night, I was so frustrated with the process that I came home to my friend's house and collapsed on the floor, crying and crying for hours. If I was not at a networking event, I was literally pounding on companies' doors inquiring about job vacancies. I needed money to simply exist and it felt like there was nothing more that I could do. After cleaning myself up from crying, I ventured upstairs to change clothes, only to discover that the portable closet had plummeted as a result of the clothing's weight. After working for an hour or so to reassemble the portable closet, I went to bed for the evening. For the next month, life's grievances became progressively worse, and mysteriously, so did the portable closet. At that point the moveable rack was falling every other day.

It seemed that for every trial I faced, this portable closet would serve as a physical manifestation of where I was in life. The weight of the world was on my shoulders and forced me into a state of deterioration. On one particular evening, I knew that something had to change in my life in order for me to simply continue existing. As the closet collapsed for the last time, I ventured into my friend's bedroom, fell to my knees, and was silent. I could not shed another tear. I was not able to utter another lament for help. My SOS plea for relief was no longer aiding me. I heard my friend come into the dark room to check on me. For the first couple of minutes, she stood at the doorway in silence. She eventually came over to where I was crouched on the floor, placed her hand on my shoulder, and said, "Klay, let it go." In that instant, I uttered one last prayer and decided to surrender to God—the Universe—to allow the Supreme Being to take on the burden that was threatening my existence.

In my experience, surrendering to a higher power can sometimes be difficult and require the continuous work of perfecting how to release. Methods such as meditation, prayer, exercise, writing, singing, dancing, and silence are potential activities that are freeing agents for clients that I work with. What technique gives you a sense of peace? Discovering your releasing agent is very critical in mastering the art of surrendering and can potentially be your saving grace in other areas of human engagement. Once I reached a state of physical, mental, emotional, and spiritual exhaustion, I was forced to surrender through the form of prayer. As a result of my need to control 'life,' I lost sight of what was important, and I could have prevented this form of self-destruction by simply trusting in the power that I've always believed in. This power has always supported my dreams and me.

Why do we try to find new ways of discovering comfort in our lives, or new avenues for obtaining dreams, success, and conquering agents of our fears, when the same mechanism that has always sustained us is the *same* force that always will? Attempting to go beyond the idea of surrendering can feel like a war of duality being waged within us. We might feel our hearts tugging in one direction for something (maybe it's unclear as to what this "power" is) to take over the burden causing us strife while in pursuit of our Plan A. On the other hand, releasing control to a being that we cannot physically see is the other difficulty. Two powerful structures are in play:

1. Our need to control, and

2. A Universal force begging us to place our life in its hand.

The difficulty with surrendering in this phase is trust. Our Plan A is so important that it almost becomes an obsession to bring it to fruition. And the one question that plagues most of our minds is, "Who can I trust more than myself to win and deliver my Plan A?" I can definitely

## CHAPTER 13: I SURRENDER ALL

relate to this question, especially as I possess a strong Type A personality—needing to be in control, organized, ready, and prepared for the task at hand. However, at the precise moment of utter internal distress, exhaustion beyond human comprehension, and deliverance of a work ethic that is our very best, there's nothing left to do but surrender.

That day in my friend's apartment was one of the first times that I understood the need to release, the need to trust, and the responsibility to my Plan A that I had to protect. Shortly after releasing my Plan A to the Universe, I received a phone call with an opportunity to work at a mission agency. Help was here. It finally came. Ironically, it was sent to me at the moment that I needed assistance the most, and at the point of my release. I did not have an inkling how this opportunity would support my Plan A, but after all that I had experienced up until this point in my life, I knew that I could trust that God was preparing me for something that I would need within the process to get to my end result.

Surrender the uttermost secret place where your passion resides, the very essence of your dream, and the capsule of your heart's deepest longings. There is a helping agent, a freeing source, and unlimited supplier who is ready to carry the torch of life for us, until ultimately the cauldron of our Plan A is lit and willing to burn until our time on earth expires.

# CONCLUSION

**Dear God,**

*The day began kind of late for me. I rested very well and ran a lot of errands on today. I also went to dinner and a movie to see The Bucket List. When you sit down and truly asks yourself about what things you would like to accomplish, experience and share, it sort of gets you thinking about your own life. So I've made this journey to New York. This excited me! I finally decided to do it! I totally stepped out on pure faith…*

# CHAPTER 14:
# I'M COMING HOME

*Question: What could really happen in your life, if you realized that out of billions and billions of people, only you can do what you were born to do? Answer: Amazing things beyond human comprehension!*

God. Powerful. Resilient. Amazing. Talented. Purpose. Centered. Humbled. Thankful. Value. Belief. Compassion. Perseverance. Optimism. Vision. Ready. When you left your space of disillusioned comfort to embark upon the adventurous terrain of Plan A, it was my hope that there would be a shift in your consciousness. It is now time for you to intentionally leave the world of fear that has not allowed you to be your true authentic self, and return home. Home is the place that once propelled you to reach greater heights of success and a juxtaposition of the spiritual, mental, physical, and emotional space of being.

Do you remember having excitement for living and functioning within your day-to-day life—the dynamic drive that you once felt not only to dream but to actually arrive at the end of that experience with a sense of joy? This sense of being is a special gift, supernatural sensation, and unlimited source to all who seek out its truth. Returning to this place of boldness is where we were always meant to gather and thrive. The Universe has sanctioned us to be unwavering examples to the world, and through your courage you will change the lives of others—many of whom you may never meet. As a result of your decision to walk in your purpose and calling, your spirit offers an energy source that is felt around the world. The idea of "paying something forward" is what you are sharing at this moment. You choose to pay forward the principles of Plan A, and thus will spiritually release vibrations of hope toward others who are seeking to recognize, accept, and fulfill their purpose as well. The effects are transmissible, and because we exist within a revolving world, our expressions are not only given to others, but will ultimately return to us in the spirit that our thoughts were shared.

Coming home does not mean that we will never experience forms of resistance within our Plan A, but it does say that we have decided to venture along a scarcely traveled path that is personal and special to each one of us. The sensation of living a life engrossed with purpose and commitment is the greatest emotion we could ever receive and give back to God, the universal guidance that first believed in us.

My Plan A journey has led me to write this book and begin teaching others how to discover their purpose and calling, and offering sustaining measures to cope with the journey toward living life as a reflection of the universal source that wants nothing but the best for each of us. This book has allowed me to share experiences and growth cycles that were vital for becoming the person that I am today. As I look back and reflect on the earlier years of my journey, I now know that there were no mistakes ever committed within my experience. While I am not perfect, I now understand that the Plan A journey *is* perfect, without fault or guilt. Plan A has taught me that there is nothing that we could ever experience in life that is not setting us up for a higher place of dignity, acceptance, advancement, and joy—if only we look for the blessing in the charge at hand.

Levels of resistance, confusion, and pain are real expressions that we will inescapably experience along our individual voyages. However, when you are authentically existing within your element and wholeheartedly allowing yourself to be used as a representation of God, a sentiment of genuine pleasure will ultimately arise that can never be taken away. Therefore, when forms of resistance and conditions occur that threaten our trust of fulfilling our Plan A, we will already know of a secret place

## CHAPTER 14: I'M COMING HOME

in our hearts that is here to sustain us—our home. Our Plan A home is a space that can never be destroyed or compromised. Forces outside of our control may attempt to intimidate this special place, but once we agree to connect with the Universe, our home will always protect and exist, calling us to a place of excellence.

Our journeys will never be over, as every day we are called to reach new heights within our purpose. I am not at the place where my dreams and visions have taken me in my heart and mind, but of course I will be. This book is a manifestation of my Plan A working on my behalf as I seek to serve others in the world. Availing to Plan A has allowed me to receive miracles each and every day, with continuous confirmation that I am on the correct trek. Regardless of how minute or grand each phenomenon might be, the sense of experiencing "the unexplainable" forces me to continue on this journey and trust the Universe to direct my actions.

Landing in a space of home has altered my sense of love for myself. For the first time in life, I can actually gaze in a mirror and say, "I love you," without a retort beginning with "but," "however," or "if only." The feeling is tangible. My emotions are factual, felt, and faithfully shared with others I come in contact with. Falsehoods of not being good enough, incapable, and unworthy cease to exist, as expressions of "I am more than," "I can," "I will," and "I am able" have taken residence in my life. Without reaching this space of internal love along the path to Plan A, there would unfortunately be no way that I could sincerely present this platform to others who are seeking forms of clarity in their life.

Plan A has taught me the importance of existing in a place of stillness, peace, and patience. Now, instead of rushing through phases that are meant to be enjoyable, I know how to be present within each moment, recognizing the importance of each event that occurs in my life. The moment that I seek to accomplish has become a part of me and offers newfound insights that are everlasting.

Coming home and living within Plan A has challenged me to offer my very best to myself, humanity, and God in whatever form of engagement that I choose to take part in. My desire to strive for distinction is no longer an impossible and far-reaching goal of attainment, but is natural and a part of my lived experience. There is a new awareness of confidence that reflects through my internal and external being. I am whole and complete, all on my own, and I take pride in how I present myself to world.

Home is a place where gratitude is offered to respectable, honest, and supporting friendships that strengthen and challenge me. Their love and countless showmanship of belief in my Plan A have allowed me to endure the pathway that I am called to accomplish. The community of hope and divine guiding forces that lives within each Plan A friendship also lives within me. Collectively, we inspire others to pursue their dreams.

My Plan A home has allowed me to surrender uncertainties, weariness, and the vision of satisfying the work that I have been allocated to perform. Surrendering is the epicenter of Plan A's home and it reassures me that every level of advancement will transpire within the Universe's perfect timing. My tireless work is fruitful, effective, and an expression of the authoritative spirit that lives at the center of my being. I can graciously and humbly relinquish my Plan A to a higher power that will toil on my behalf.

We have arrived at a home that is forgiving. Plan A offers grace and mercy to others for offenses that are committed against us. Not only does our new home absolve others, this space also liberates us from occurrences that are not favorable in our eyes—ill feelings of discomfort that we have internally embraced as self-hate throughout our existence. We are healed and beautiful, and command a space that says, "I am enough." In turn, we understand the healing power that the world demands from us.

The foundation which each of us was produced upon is one of the most dynamic forms of love that the Universe has granted us. At the core of our naked souls are gifts with immeasurable potential to change our lives and the world around us. Today, the world is begging for us to walk in self-assurance and power that we all possess. The only way we could ever possibly fail is if we do not operate in the rich consciousness, spirit, and present state of living out our Plan A that we have been called

## CHAPTER 14: I'M COMING HOME

to perform. It is time to reposition our lives that lethargically exist on the margins of time and powerfully embrace the fullness of our Plan A. How many more miracles and green and red flags must happen for us to simply believe in ourselves, believe that we all have a special Plan A, and believe that something higher than ourselves seeks to give us this knowledge?

The world is begging for new-age leaders to rise and take part in the flow of life. More importantly, the world needs us to rise. We have an obligation to the Universe and to the children that are coming along in a complex world, where dreams are never heard or expressed, and are simply ignored. The Universe does not need time to work out who we were meant to be. The responsibility lies within you and I.

Come home and allow the Universe to initiate in you an enormous, sustaining, loving, and eternal work. The question that quiets the mind, excites the soul, invigorates the body, and that will begin to channel the direction of your Plan A is:

"God, what is my special task that you ask of me to perform?" There, home awaits.

# APPENDIX:
## PLAN A APHORISMS

Give to others forgiveness and in turn, the Universe will give you back your life.

Patience is a virtue that will never set us up for failure.

I was greeted this morning with the most amazing sunshine, torrential outpouring of joy spilling over from my very soul, and a message from the universe kindly whispering, "Let me be your angel...." And I gladly accepted its request.

I'm going to trust what's happening and not get in the way of the force that's called "Life."

Simply be...still.

I am always at the right place, at the right time

What could really change in your life, if one day you simply decided that you were "enough"?

What could really happen if for once in your life you decided to venture on a bold new path? You know, the one less traveled. What new things could you experience? What could you learn about yourself? Who could you potentially become? Who could you inspire to follow their life's dreams? Take just one bold step and find out.

After you've done all that you can, don't just 'stand,' but SURRENDER and allow the process to construct the 'how' for you.

It's never my job to tell people what they should believe or not, but having faith in something aside ourselves makes life a tad bit easier.

Let the light of another day be enough.

Each experience in life is a steppingstone toward something great, if you trust the process. Besides, the adventure is so much more fun when you do!

Unless you're prepared to deal with "Negative Nellies," keep your dreams close (with like-minded friends) until they manifest. Try showing up and making announcements rather than asking so many negative and fearful people their thoughts about your dream!

It's hard not to focus on the structure or foundation of a dream that we're hoping to create. Structures give us a sense of stability and confidence. However, sometimes it's more important to pay closer attention to each layer of the structure, precisely placing each brick in its intended place. Who knows? The foundation may be better than what you ever could have imagined.

Aren't you tired of being someone that you're clearly not? "But the road to success is…" is what you've been telling yourself. No, the road to success is governed and "sustained" by those who are authentically themselves. Give it a try and watch unopened doors suddenly appear to be available in every direction you turn. Dare to not be 'ordinary.'

"Oh, they're just so lucky," we say to ourselves as we watch friends or total strangers in careers that we want, living a life that we long to live, and creatively expressing new ideas and thoughts. "Why them? Why not me? I work hard!" you might say to yourself. Well, the only course of action that is different is that they believe in their dream and you do not. Dreams without true belief are empty and cannot come to fruition.

The feeling becomes overwhelming when you have a date with destiny, but at the 11th hour, you must dig deep inside to continue. What you need is *perserverance*.

Whatever it is, love is the cure.

Your target is in sight. Your dream has surfaced right before your very eyes. Yet, a very eager enemy ties you to a chair and renders you voiceless. Its name is resistance. Know this voice. Then remember your true inner voice and courageously run on to your destiny.

Authenticity wins the race.

My Universe is very protective, so watch out!

Dreams fulfilled require us to operate from a place of complete, unrelenting, and unapologetic AUTHORITY.

Authentic friendships do not require an explanation of why you want a better life...they just support it.

God's gift of true friendship is one of the most amazing gifts I've ever experienced. My relationships with friends have not only added substance to my life, but as a result, I am closer to God because of the experience.

To be embraced by life means first knowing that I embrace myself.

Jealousy gets us nowhere. If people have something that you desire, a skill that you'd like to hone, or a gift or talent that you've come to admire, ask them how they got to where they are. Chances are they could help strengthen and charge your path with an extra boost of optimism and enhanced vision. Celebrate, so when it's your turn, others will celebrate with and on behalf of you.

Sometimes losing control is the quickest method to finding our sanity.

*THERE IS ONLY PLAN A*

You have to appreciate and find gratitude for the race and challenges of life in the valley, as much as the amazing reward of reaching the Mountaintop!

There is only Plan A! And because there is only Plan A, there's no reason why your God-given dream cannot come true.

The 'there and then' we are looking for is lodged in the 'here and now.'

It's not magic! It's good energy, faith, and determination!

Ultimately, it is the risk of courage that offers advancement toward true self-enlightenment.

The more I understand that I'm responsible for my happiness, the greater my desire becomes to surround myself with other joy-seeking individuals. This is the part of life we can control.

The gift of being there for friends, helping them dream, vision, and believe, is the greatest experience of love one can receive.

I'm committed to making this moment the best time of my life...just because I want it to be.

I am celebrating now for one of the most exciting ventures I will experience in my life. It's already here, so why not?

Instead of responding with, "Why?" "How?" and "Are you sure?" maybe the correct response is, "Thank you!" Gratitude goes a long way and pays your next visit of kindness forward.

The quickest method to approaching disaster is thinking you're moving forward, while looking back.

It's okay to get angry at life. Have your moment, but never forget that the same energy force that brought you through the 15 million other times will be the same power that will bring you through yet again. God is here.

Surrendering and asking the Universe to prepare in us a work that is ours and ours alone propels us to a new form of consciousness.

Today I will be all that I've been destined to become, one moment at a time, one setback at a time, one form of resistance at a time. And one dream, all along the way.

*(Stepping up to the batter's plate):* "It's my turn!"

A part of moving beyond our former relationships and attracting a newfound love is in understanding that our mates will reveal themselves to us, when we stop looking to our past in both memory and deed.

The great thing about rejection is that it gets rid of the mediocre opportunities that stand in the way of the great victory attempting to find us!

Question whether it will rain today or tomorrow, but not if you deserve the life that the unlimited source has in store for you.

Even in the most trying situations, life is setting you up for something greater than you could ever imagine, if only you believe.

And today, a great portion of my personal Plan A has come true. And greatness thereafter goes to the benefit of a loving, gracious, and just Universe.

I will seek not my own understanding, but the understanding, dreams, and livelihood that only God can give me. And so it is.

Quietness and silence are always perfect indicators for authentic transformation. Be quiet.

The sooner we learn how to release our need to control, the sooner our life's direction will begin to run its authentic course.

"No! I choose me." New things can and will happen as a result of your bravery.

Waking up to the feeling that your area of work has value, betters the world, and the human condition is the greatest feeling!

If you are person trying to find your purpose based on human and earthly achievements, you will fail.

In the end, a firm "No" to others will bring a sweet "Yes" to you and your quality of life!

Destiny will always kiss the lips of those who are open to its call.

Whenever authenticity is lived, it opens the door for life to bring us the good stuff.

Purpose is often found when we exercise and strengthen our muscle of awareness. What is life trying to show you? Go with it.

The victory is always sweeter when you've perspired a bit for its realization.

Made in the USA
Lexington, KY
29 March 2014